VIKINGS IN NORTH WEST ENGLAND

Vikings in North West England

The Artifacts

B. J. N. Edwards

Centre for North-West Regional Studies
University of Lancaster
1998

Vikings in North West England

This volume is the 36th in a series published by the Centre for North-West Regional Studies at the University of Lancaster.

Editorial Board: Elizabeth Roberts, David Shotter, Angus Winchester

Text copyright © B. J. N. Edwards, 1998

Published by the Centre for North-West Regional Studies, University of Lancaster

Designed and typeset by Carnegie Publishing Ltd,
Carnegie House, Chatsworth Road, Lancaster LA1 4SL

Printed and bound in the UK by Redwood Books, Wilts

British Library Cataloguing-in-Publication Data
A CIP catalogue record for this book is available from the British Library
ISBN 1-86220-065-3

Contents

List of Illustrations

All photographs are by the author, as are all drawings except where otherwise noted.

Foreword

The project of which this book represents a final stage began more years ago than I care to remember as an idea for some work for an afternoon not otherwise very busy. It was to be no more than a mapping exercise, with the intention of plotting all known find spots of Viking artifacts between Dee and Solway and west of the watershed. The innocence with which that was undertaken is an index of how little I knew of the subject at the time. It soon became evident, as it should have been from the outset, that to map information of this kind one must first cull it from a wide variety of sources. That I have been doing, in one way or another, ever since.

When the material was more or less assembled, and capable of being used, for example for lectures, it occurred to me that it might be useful to have it on paper for other people's use. Since its geographical coverage did not coincide with those of archaeological societies, the Centre for North West Regional Studies seemed to be the obvious outlet. Since then, its Directors have waited patiently for its arrival, and indeed the Director who first approved the idea has moved on to other fields. I can only commend the patience of Marion McClintock and Elizabeth Roberts.

Somewhere during the gestation period of this work occurred the 150th anniversary of the discovery of the Cuerdale Hoard, in 1990, which was marked by an Exhibition and a Conference at Liverpool Museum. The bare bones of my material were given as a lecture at the Conference and appeared in the volume which resulted. For asking me to give that lecture, editing it for the volume, and much other help at various times, I am delighted to thank Professor James Graham Campbell.

The mention of three names as recipients of my gratitude might be the occasion for a flood of names to follow. Were I to attempt to make such a list of people who have helped me to assemble this study, it would be, first, too long, and, second, invidious in its inclusions and its omissions. Anyone who has lived with a subject for a long time will know how dependent one is on others' generosity, and how frequently it is forthcoming. Suffice it to say, then, that I am grateful to many people, none of whom is responsible for the idiosyncracies of the way in which I have used their material.

The only exception to my avoidance of naming names in the matter of help must be that of my wife, Margaret, whose question 'How are the Vikings getting on?' has spurred me on many times. I can only hope that she thinks the result is worth it.

CHAPTER ONE

Introductory

'The Vikings', said David Wilson, 'had a bad press'. It was inevitable that it should be so, for those who had suffered most at their hands were the only literate members of the community. Of recent years it has become a commonplace to reject the view of the Vikings propounded by the church, which was scarcely unbiased, or at least to temper that view with wise and sober comments on the polemical exaggeration of clerical reports of Viking depredations, or on the Vikings' virtues as travellers, traders and craftsmen.

If we seek a balanced view, we come, inevitably, to the question of terminology. In the expression made famous by Dr Joad of the Radio *Brains Trust*, 'It depends what you mean by a Viking'. That the first raiders who appeared on the eastern shores of Britain in the late eighth century were justly feared there is no doubt. Similarly, there is little doubt about the intentions of the Danes' 'Great Army'; they were undoubtedly different from those of the raiders, but they were none the less hostile. By contrast, the nature and intentions of those Vikings who were responsible for the evidence to be considered in these pages were arguably very different. Some, at least, of them were refugees, and others, it has been argued, came with such peaceful intent that they accepted those areas of land not already settled by people of Celtic or Germanic origin, and therefore probably less favourable for settlement.

What, then, in that case, do all these raiders and settlers have in common? In a word, the answer is 'Scandinavia'. Even the authenticity of the famous litany of appeal for deliverance from the fury of the Northmen is now denied; but Northmen is what they were to

the established population of Britain. Again, however, the degree of connection, the closeness of association, with the northern homelands varied. Most of the 'Danes' who first attacked, and then settled in, eastern England were at least born in Scandinavia, some, of course in what we now call Sweden rather than Denmark. But of how many settlers in western Britain it can be said that more than their ancestry was Scandinavian is another matter. They and their ancestors had spent a generation or two in the Western Isles, in Ireland or in Man.

We know that some Norse or Vikings came to parts of the north west of England early in the tenth century. The source is not impeccable, but 'Ingimund's Invasion' of Wirral, as Wainwright called it (Wainwright 1948 = Wainwright 1975 (ed. Finberg) 131–162)), is not seriously doubted. This sole piece of documentary evidence for Norse settlement in north west England has produced a tendency for writers to assume that all Norse place-name evidence and all Viking artifacts from Dee to Solway date from this period at the earliest. The datable documentary tail has wagged the less precisely datable archaeological and toponymic dog.

There are hints that this is not the true picture. Some of the artifacts and their deposition in furnished (and therefore, presumably, pagan) graves suggest earlier activity, within the ninth century. The shield boss in the Ormside burial (p. 18) is a case in point. Indeed, the presence of so many furnished graves in itself suggests that there may well have been substantial settlement in the area before the early tenth century, by which time Christianity might be expected to be general. True, we know that the Vikings had their equivalents of what were known in early Chinese missionary circles as 'rice Christians', and approaching death does tend to turn men away from a religion to which they have been converted back to that in which they were nurtured. Nevertheless, the process of conversion to Christianity is complete in a generation or so, and the suspicion remains that ninth century Norse activity may have been more prevalent in the area than has been hitherto conceded.

Given the comparatively small volume of material, and the difficulties in its dating, together with the almost total lack of documentary references to the area, what is it possible to make of the way in which settlement took place? Facts which give at least some ideas can be cited. For example, that personal names of Scandinavian origin were in widespread use after the Norman Conquest argues that the influence was comprehensive. So, too, do such pointers as the language used in the runic inscription on the Pennington tympanum. The deposit within our area of the Cuerdale Hoard must have some implications, and the precise location of its findspot on the route between the Norse kingdoms of York and Dublin suggests that some form of intercourse passed between them through the area.

We have already started, however, to consider our subject with the background knowledge produced by nearly a century and a half of research. It behoves us to pause and consider what prompted this research, the initiation of which it is so easy to take for granted. From our point of view it is perhaps fortuitous that much of the early impetus for putting archaeological studies in general on a systematic basis took place in Scandinavia. Partly at least as a result of this, Scandinavian scholars, already better versed in the fundamentals of archaeology than most, began to look towards the British Isles, some of them with a view to comparing material found in their home areas with that found further afield, and in particular to look for and study specifically Scandinavian remains found in Britain and Ireland.

Earliest of these was J. J. A. Worsaae, who was sent by the King of Denmark to visit these islands in 1846–47. That visit resulted in a book, *An Account of the Danes and Norwegians in England, Scotland and Ireland,* published in 1852. This, as its title makes clear, was a wide-ranging study, but it was followed only four years later by a regional study specifically restricted to the northern part of our region. This was '*The Northmen in Cumberland and Westmorland*' by Robert Ferguson (1856) and it is interesting to look at the nature of the evidence he cites.

In a book of eleven chapters and well over 200 pages, only two chapters, totalling twenty-five pages, even purport to deal with what we might recognise today as archaeology, and, of these, the seventeen pages of the chapter entitled 'Sepulchral Remains of the Northmen' include a brief description only of the burial at Beacon Hill, Aspatria. No other truly archaeological sites are discussed, and the remainder of the chapter, like most of the six other chapters, relies for its evidence on some very hit-or-miss place-name etymology.

Thus, lists of 'barrow' names from Anglebarrow to Whitbarrow are considered as the burial places of Norsemen from Angel to Hvti. Again, '-how' names (Blackhow to Wad's How) are traced to men named Blaka to Vadi, and even 'hills' are pressed into service with such names as Beacon Hill and Mill Hill being attributed to Bekan and Miöll. A large portion of the chapter is taken up with an extended discussion of the derivation of the name Kirrock. When an attempt *was* made to cite graves in which 'arms have been found', the author was at the mercy of contemporary lack of knowledge by which to date them. Thus, a grave on Sandford Moor, 'opened' in 1766, was furnished with an urn containing ashes with a smaller example within it, together with a sword and other items. We can say that there is not much doubt that this was a Bronze Age burial with an urn and an accessory vessel and so forth, but how was Ferguson to know?

Similarly, the chapter on runic inscriptions, having begun rather wistfully by reporting that the runes on the Ruthwell and Bewcastle crosses, though once claimed as Scandinavian, had by then been firmly established as Anglo-Saxon, goes on to dismiss other crosses in Cumberland which might well have helped the author's case. These, he says, 'have scrolls, figures and ornaments interlaced similar to the monuments of Norwegian origin in the Isle of Man'. Here his courage, so widely displayed in guesswork on place-names, failed him. 'The resemblance', he wrote, 'between the Scotch and Scandinavian monuments is such as to prevent us, in the absence of any inscription, from forming any decisive opinion as to their origin'. Thereafter, he could cite only two runic inscriptions, that on the font at Bridekirk and the 'Dolfin' runes, then recently discovered in Carlisle Cathedral, both of which we now know to be post-Conquest. It is, perhaps, surprising, given the state of knowledge in the middle of the nineteenth century, that Ferguson got as close to the truth in general terms as he did.

The contributions of later nineteenth and early twentieth century workers such as W. S. Calverley and W. G. Collingwood, though not confined to sculpture, are considered in the chapter on that subject.

Although, as far as possible, this account of the Vikings in north west England will deal in facts, we must also consider at least one very pervasive piece of fiction, or at least fictionalised fact. This relates to the Battle of Brunanburh (Campbell (ed.) 1938, 43–160), which seems to have taken place in AD 937, involving an army of Anglo-Saxons (West Saxons and Mercians) under the leadership of Athelstan and his brother, Edmund. They were responding to an attack by a mixed force of Norsemen and Scots led by Anlaf and Constantine, King of Scots. These latter had come by ship, penetrated deep into English territory, taken much booty and been little resisted, as a result, we are told, of a Saxon plan. Ultimately, the Saxon army forced the invaders to abandon much of their booty and flee back to their ships.

They escaped to Dublin, and this fact, combined with the general situation in north west England, has led many people to assert that the battle took place in that area. One (late) source which makes the invaders land in the Humber estuary has slightly weakened the case for this, but what is often forgotten is that the whole episode is known to us only from poetic sources. True, the poems are quoted by 'historians' of the early medieval period (anonymous annalists, William of Malmesbury, Florence (John) of Worcester) but they had neither the training nor the apparatus to be critical of their sources. As a result, much ink has been spilt (e.g. Dodgson 1956–7) in attempts to identify the places named, particularly Brunanburh itself, and the types of landscapes described or implied by the poem. Among the many candidates are Burnswark in Dumfriesshire, Burnley and the shore near Blackpool in Lancashire and Bromborough in Cheshire.

The latter might be thought to have the best claim, in that respected place-name scholars have asserted that the early forms of the name Bromborough prove that the earliest form of the name was indeed Brunanburh. Even this, of course, proves nothing, since there might well have been more than one place with the same name. Attractive though the game is, we must ultimately admit that, without some more reliable corroboration, the actual tale of the Battle of Brunanburh and its preceding campaign must be accounted no more than a good story. The inclusion of the named battle in northern versions of the Anglo-Saxon Chronicle makes the battle's actual occurrence highly probable, but the details of that battle and its location cannot be pinned down with the sources at present available.

Before we consider very briefly what we can deduce about the impact of the Scandinavians on the region, as we can reconstruct it from the evidence cited in the following chapters, there are a few other matters which require comment.

Chief among these is the matter of the two ancient cities at the extreme ends of the region. Chester and Carlisle are similar in that each began as a Roman site, different in precise origin. Each can also demonstrate late pre-Conquest occupation, but neither has yielded substantial Viking remains. It may well be that the explanation of this lies in the fact that the Norwegians who came to north west England were not town-dwellers and therefore that their settlements were largely rural. Even the existence of the Viking town at Dublin (from which, apparently, some at least of our settlers came) is no more than the exception which proves the rule.

At Chester, excavations in Lower Bridge Street revealed the post-holes of what were interpreted as cellared buildings of the tenth century. Despite the claim in the Foreword to the report (Mason 1985, iii) that this was proof of the fact that Chester had Vikings, the finds associated with the buildings were meagre and, of these, only a stone ingot-mould looks as though it might have Viking associations. The specialist report on this object, however, having cited finds elsewhere of both moulds and ingots, suggests that cigar-shaped ingots were 'a normal part of the equipment for non-ferrous metalworking rather than [being] specifically associated with Viking raiders'. The general conclusion was that the tenth century buildings were more likely to have been part of the Athelfledan *burh*. All of this has the attraction of being in general agreement with the *Three Fragments* account of what happened to Ingimund and his Hiberno-Norse refugees. The coin hoards found at various dates in Chester (detailed in Chapter four) of course necessarily suggest no more than trade between Norse and Saxon.

Carlisle, too, seems equally reluctant to produce clear evidence of occupation which appears to have any Scandinavian connotations. Despite the presence of Anglian sculpture, and evidence of Norse sculpture and burials not very far away (for example at Stanwix and Hesket-in-the-Forest (below, p. 10–14)), no Norse sculpture has been recorded in the city, and, similarly, few other relevant artifacts seem to have been discovered in the course of quite extensive excavations in recent years.

It may, of course, be the case that, at both of the cities of Chester and Carlisle, an area of Norse occupation may lie where it happens to have been missed by excavation, but the sparseness of casual finds in both cities makes this seem unlikely. In the case of Carlisle, indeed, the alleged sacking of the city in the last quarter of the ninth century under Halfdan, king at York, may go some away to explain the apparent lack of tenth and early eleventh century occupation – a dearth to some extent explained by the statement of a medieval chronicler (Florence (John) of Worcester) that the city lay waste for two centuries after Halfdan's raid; however, doubt has been cast on the likelihood that the city remained derelict for so long a period.

It is interesting in this connection to note that when Carlisle again appears in history, under the Normans in the late eleventh century, it is held by a man named Dolfin, a Norse-derived name. The same name, indeed, appears in a *graffito* in runes within the Cathedral of Carlisle. Without necessarily being references to the same man, they do at least remind us of the pervasiveness of Scandinavian names, writing methods and, probably, language into a period beyond the scope of this book.

If the lack of much evidence for Norse settlement in two cities may be explained by the idea that the Scandinavian peoples were country dwellers, the material remains of their presence may be under many a village with a Scandinavian-based name. Not every village with a name which appears, at first glance, to be of Scandinavian derivation was necessarily a Viking settlement. Nevertheless, there is a great density of place names containing Norse elements in north west England. A map of Scandinavian-based place names in England shows a greater density in eastern Yorkshire, Lincolnshire, Leicestershire and Nottinghamshire. The majority of these, however, are of Danish origin rather than Norse.

Many, if not most, of the names represented today by villages will have begun as tiny settlements, farmsteads or little more. It is one of the frustrations of the archaeology of this period that, if only we knew precisely – that is, to a very few square yards – where to look, we could probably uncover the remains of one of these Viking settlements. Since we do not, and the material remains are not likely to be such as to catch the eye of house builders, drain layers or gardeners, we do not have any direct evidence as to what was represented by all these place names.

Not every settlement grew into a village, however. We can still find farms whose names are constructed with the same elements and in the same way as those of villages. There, too, below ground evidence must survive, but it is not readily accessible. It lies either under the existing farmstead or somewhere else in the vicinity where its presence cannot be traced. Where Viking farms have been excavated, either in this country or in Scandinavia, their excavation took place because the farmstead never developed further and so had left visible traces at ground level.

Such a site, only just outside our region, was that at Ribblehead in Yorkshire (King 1978), which has become enshrined in the literature as that of a Viking farm. It must be said that the evidence for this classification is relatively slight. It is not to be doubted that the long house (the two unhyphenated words show that no technical use is here implied) was occupied at the relevant period and that

coin evidence showed connection with the Viking town of York (specifically, coins of the Viking archbishop, Plegmund). What was noticeable was a lack of distinctively Scandinavian artifacts. However, this is perhaps not surprising. After all, a look at the finds from the known Viking occupation levels at York would show many which were not distinctively Scandinavian. Thus, given the very small total of finds from such a site as Ribblehead, the presence among them of recognisable Viking artifacts would be a fairly long chance indeed.

Given this analysis of an accepted Viking rural site, we can now turn to the only similar site so far excavated in the north west of England. High in Kentmere, on the side of a tributary valley, lie the remains of the building known by the name of that stream, Bryant's Gill (Dickinson 1985). Like Ribblehead, it was occupied for a long enough period for modifications in the building to have taken place. Again like Ribblehead, the yield of finds from the excavation was small. This is entirely to be expected, given the likely lowly status of the inhabitants of such a remote site and the poor conditions for preservation probable in moorland areas. The finding of such objects as whetstones and spindle whorls is exactly as expected on such a site, yet would be probable had the site been occupied at any time from the Bronze Age to the post-medieval period. The questions which have to be answered from *our* point of view are: first, does the totality of the evidence – site, shape of building, nature of finds – make it seem likely that the building derives from the two or three centuries with which we are concerned; and, second, if so, does that evidence include any specific Norse or Viking elements? The answers seem to be positive to the first question, less certain to the second, though a parallel has been drawn between spindle whorls from Kentmere and examples from the Viking settlement of Hedeby, north Germany. Bryant's Gill, like Ribblehead, is beginning to be accepted as a Viking rural settlement.

Another characteristic of Viking life which has left evidence in the place names is that of community organisation. For instance, one of the best known Viking sites in the Isle of Man is the mount at Tynwald, where the 'thing', or assembly, met, and there is evidence to show that it was by no means a unique feature in Viking communities. It has, however, been preserved and tidied up by long continuous use. There is a candidate in north west England for inclusion in this class of site, too, though it looks somewhat different. This is the terraced rectangular mound in Little Langdale. One has to say that little more can be done than to describe the site and leave it to readers' judgement as to whether or not it is what had been suggested.

This type of site is not one where excavation, even if it were possible, would be likely to answer many questions. Datable evidence, still less racially or nationally distinctive evidence, would be extremely unlikely to be found under or in a mound constructed solely to provide an elevated area. One could argue that prolonged use would inevitably result in the deposition, at least by loss, of some artifacts, but recovering any of them would be a very different matter.

Before leaving the question of the Little Langdale site, we can make the same observation as is often produced by remarkable archaeological discoveries: if it is not what is suggested, what on earth is it? The explanation of a terraced garden seems to be in the highest degree unlikely. Terraced gardens tend to go down rather than up from the general surrounding level, and, in any case, elaborate gardens of this kind are not probable in such a location. W. G. Collingwood himself was convinced, and even if we ourselves are perhaps a little more cautious, we may recall that real advances in understanding are often made by men who are prepared to stick their necks out.

What, then, was the impact – the effect – of the arrival in north west England of settlers of Scandinavian descent between, perhaps,

the late ninth and the mid tenth centuries? It was, we must say at once, considerable. This is clear from the many traces which have survived. Archaeological evidence is discussed with some attempt at completeness in the following pages: only sculpture, of the various classes of objects considered, is ubiquitous enough to be dealt with without mentioning every piece, otherwise all the evidence of this kind is dealt with.

It would be interesting if we could discern enough of life in the area immediately prior to the Viking incursions to be able to demonstrate precisely the changes resulting from those incursions. This we cannot do. The situation is somewhat similar to that half a millennium earlier. We did not have direct Anglo-Saxon invasion as did many areas of the eastern side of England. We do not have a rich Anglo-Saxon archaeological record as do many of those areas – Northumbria and its predecessors, Deira and Bernicia particularly. And yet the Anglo-Saxons were here in the north west of England in some force. They left place names and sculpture, if relatively little else, but other Anglo-Saxon objects crept westward to places like Birdoswald. But in truth, even in the archaeologically rich areas of Anglo-Saxon northern England we have comparatively little evidence for everyday life. Just as we can discern little of what life was like for the immediately post-Roman inhabitants of the area before Anglo-Saxon influence changed it, so the change from Anglo-Saxon predominance to Norse is difficult to pin down.

It certainly seems probable that the Norse influence on the, presumably, mixed British and Germanic population of north west England was more all-pervasive than the Germanic influence had been on the native population in the early post-Roman period. Of course, being later, its traces in such matters as names is likely to be more lasting. But there has been plenty of time since for other factors to change the situation. The fact remains, however, that vast numbers of natural features retain Scandinavian names, as do many villages. Much has also survived in such relatively minor matters as dialect. Stories have been told of men from the north west precipitated by the accidents of military service to Iceland and claiming to have been able to make themselves understood. No doubt an element of exaggeration has crept in here, but the presence in that country of fells called by that name and waterfalls called – foss must at least have reduced their feelings of homesickness. They call to mind suggestions made fairly recently that the Scandinavian invaders of the late first millennium may have been at least partly able to communicate with the Anglo-Saxons whom they found here.

But in truth what one can say without fear of contradiction is that the arrival of Norsemen in our area had a considerable effect on culture, in the widest sense of that word, and that that effect is a potent element among the rich mixture of influences which have fashioned the way men have lived in the area in the succeeding thousand years or so.

Finally in this chapter, a couple of minor mysteries. The Cuerdale Hoard, by far the greatest discovery of the period made in the area, in terms of value both financial and evidential, was found in 1840. And yet there is good evidence for the existence, prior to that date, of a local saying to the effect that anyone standing in the churchyard of St Leonard's church, Walton-le-Dale, and looking up the Ribble valley, was looking over the greatest treasure in Christendom. How so? Was there a folk memory of the burial of the treasure which lasted over 900 years? We can say only that we do not know, and that, like all the best mysteries, this must remain a mystery. It is no less tantalising to note that the map which accompanied T. D. Whitaker's *History of Whalley*, published in 1801, and which was repeated unchanged in later editions, shows the conventional sign for a battle (crossed swords) at or near the Cuerdale site, and that, too, is unexplained.

CHAPTER TWO

Burials

It is often the case that it is easier to recognise the traces of the death of people in the past than it is to recognise the evidence for where and how they lived. This is easily explicable by the fact that very often objects were buried with the dead, and these, when found by people with no specialist knowledge, attract attention, even if they are not understood. By contrast, the remains of domestic rubbish, which is what so much of settlement archaeology depends on, are seldom sufficiently spectacular to be noticed by other than practised eyes.

It is therefore not particularly surprising that we can point to a number of places at which evidence for Viking burials has been found, while it is well nigh impossible to point to a precise spot within the area we are dealing with and say 'A Viking lived there'. Even in the eighteenth century, long before the advent of anything we would now understand as archaeology, burial monuments attracted the attention of the curious and investigations sometimes led to the discovery of what we now know to be evidence of burials of the Viking period. It is in fact in the north west of England that we come closest to what might be called a concentration of Viking burials. Others, some of them more spectacular, are known in Ireland, Scotland and, particularly, the Isle of Man. A quarter of a century ago, when a survey of the Viking burials of England was carried out (Wilson 1967), about half of those noted were in the north west.

Given that a number of the burials were marked by some kind of visible monument – mound or cairn – it is perhaps surprising that only one seems to have been excavated

deliberately in order to find out what was in it, and that in the eighteenth century! This was at Beacon Hill, Aspatria, where there was a mound some six feet in height. Whether or not the possibility of the mound's being the remains of the Beacon from which the hill took its name had occurred to the owner of the land, Mr Rigg, we do not know. At any rate he issued instructions for the mound to be 'levelled'. Within it were found a number of large stones, a skeleton and some grave goods. The finds were drawn and reported on by Maj. Hayman Rooke (Rooke 1792).[1]

Rooke was told that the burial had been found in a 'cist' or chamber, made up of six stones, two at each side, and one each at head and foot. We are not told of any covering stones, but these there must have been, presumably. The cist lay in a mound about thirty feet in diameter and within it were the skeleton and the accompanying grave goods.

When we read an account such as this, written before the advent of scientific archaeology, it is easy to forget that facts such as sizes may not have been--as accurately measured as we would today. Add to this the fact that Maj. Rooke was working, at least as far as the excavation itself was concerned, on hearsay, and we can perhaps take with a pinch of salt the statement that the skeleton was seven feet in length from head to ankle bone. While present-day myth has it that everyone in the past was very short, the eighteenth century would have been quite happy with giants. And if the warrior buried had been a giant, so too his sword must have been appropriately long, and we are told that it was five feet long.

Although he gives a drawing of the sword,

it will certainly have been much corroded and it is wholly probable that Rooke did not see all of it. Indeed its corroded state is testified to by the fact that Rooke's drawing shows it without grip or pommel. It did, however, have a guard, and this was said to have been 'elegantly ornamented with inlaid silver flowers'. We may take leave, since he does not give us a drawing of these, to doubt Rooke's 'flowers',[2] but a guard inlaid with silver decoration is entirely probable.

The 'small knife or dagger' which was also found had a handle which 'appeared to have been studded with silver', which observation suggests that it may have been a spearhead. Apart from the silver decoration, the sword and spearhead were largely of iron, and the burial was accompanied by other items of iron. These were an axe-head, a horse's bit and a spur. All three of these objects are such as are regularly found in Viking burials, and Rooke's drawings are good enough to show that they were exactly the types of object we might expect. This is important because there were two more objects which were much more unusual, and if we can show that Rooke's illustrations of objects reasonably familiar to us (though they were not, of course, to him) are recognisable, then we must assume that his drawings of the other two objects were of much the same standard.

These two objects were a strap-end and a buckle (figure 1), but they were of gold. That they, or at least the strap-end, really consisted of gold rather than being plated or gilt we also know because the account tells us 'This

Mr Rigg proved to be gold by trying it with aquafortis'. Aquafortis should be Nitric acid, though the term is not always used with absolute precision. Nonetheless its use is scarcely a technique which would commend itself to a modern conservator! It has to be said that it is within the bounds of possibility that if Mr Rigg's acid were less than concentrated and his test less than carefully carried out, the two objects might have been gilt bronze. Either way, they were exotica in contrast to the other contents of the grave, and we must presumably see them as originating in Carolingian Europe, along with several other pieces of metalwork which we shall come across.

If the gold objects at Aspatria were unexpected, they are explicable. Equally unexpected but much less easily explained were two of the stones which made up the cist there. Their surprising characteristic was that they were decorated. One of them is shown with decoration consisting only of two sets of concentric circles, which might well be an attempt to represent cup and ring marks of the type usually attributed to the Bronze Age. If this were the case, we should assume that it was mere coincidence that a stone so marked should have been selected for use in the make-up of a Viking cist. The other stone, however, has four large and three smaller circular marks together with at least four other symbols. Of the circular symbols two large and two small have crosses in relief (and Rooke is specific about this) and the other three have a mark starting at the centre

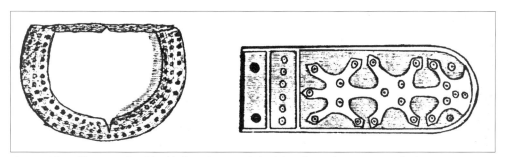

Figure 1. The gold strap-end and buckle from the Aspatria burial, as drawn for Hayman Rooke in 1792.

and protruding two or more diameters beyond the rim, giving the effect of a handle.

There is another cairn in Cumbria which has yielded large stones carrying carvings, but there does not seem to be any doubt that this was a Bronze Age burial site (it yielded two inhumations, at least 32 cremations, urns, two accessory vessels and twelve jet beads). The similarity between the carvings at this site (Old Parks, Kirkoswald (Ferguson 1856)) and those recorded at Aspatria was always slight, and really limited to one circle at Kirkoswald apparently containing a cross, but even this is not now to be found on the stone.

Three further points are worth mentioning in connection with the Aspatria burial. First, the site itself. Beacon Hill is not easy to locate on the map. The name is still in use for part of the village, and a large school also bears the name. However, the village is strung out along an east-to-west ridge, and the ground 1000 yards (900m) to the west is some bit higher than any point along the road in the vicinity of Beacon Hill School. Since one would expect a beacon to be on the highest point in the area, the location of the name seemed puzzling. Resolution of the problem was not made any easier by the fact that the 50′ contour interval of the OS 1″ map happens to obscure the situation. Ground investigation revealed the answer. Beacon Hill proper rises behind (north and west of) the School. West of Beacon Hill is a substantial valley runing northwards, but not containing a stream. Neither the hill itself nor the valley extends as far south as the main east-west road, and their presence is thus obscured when using the road. In point of fact, the ground slightly to the north of the road at the extreme west end of the parish (in the vicinity of the house called Castlemont) is slightly higher than Beacon Hill itself, but this is presumably explained by the fact that the beacon was meant to be seen to north, east and south, but not particularly to the west, where the sea is located only 4 miles (6.4km) away.

The presence or otherwise of the beacon (presumably of medieval or post-medieval date, though I cannot find it in lists of Cumbrian beacons) is, of course, irrelevant to the Norse burial, being useful only in the finding of the spot on which the burial was located. What is surprising, and constitutes the second additional fact of interest about this burial, is that the site of the barrow is perfectly visible on the ground as a circular area in which the grass is noticeably more sparse and thistles more prolific than in the surrounding areas. It is, of course, possible that the visible site is that of the beacon rather than the burial, but this does not seem probable. The third of the interesting additional facts about this burial is, like the first, tied up with nomenclature. The burial is referred to as 'Beacon Hill, Aspatria.' Among the items described in Chapter 3 below (p. 32) is a bossed penannular brooch referred to as from 'Brayton'. What these names obscure is the fact that both sites are in the same parish and a mere 1.4 miles (2.3km) apart (figure 2). Aspatria church, with its hogback and other Norse sculpture, lies about a quarter of the distance eastward from Beacon Hill towards Brayton Park Lake.

We may have been surprised that the earliest-recorded Viking burial in our area was deliberately investigated rather than discovered accidentally. Perhaps equally unexpectedly, the next two were both found in the same year, 1822, and both as a result of that quintessentially modern activity, roadworks! The earlier of the two to be discovered (Hodgson 1832), in February of that year, seems to smack of modernity also in that the roadworks in question seem hardly to have been necessary. Until then, the road, the main road from Penrith to Carlisle which we know as the A6, had a small deviation made necessary by the presence of a cairn. Much of the material of that cairn had been removed fairly recently, some for repairing field walls and some for use in the repair of the road itself, in which fate it shared with many an ancient burial cairn, they being much more convenient than a parish quarry if they lay near to a road.

When the decision was taken to straighten the road, the site of the cairn was already ploughed over, and it was presumably the preparation of the site for the new line of the road which actually revealed the remains of the burial on 5 February. The account of the discovery gives the size of the cairn as slightly smaller than that at Aspatria – 22 feet as opposed to 30 feet – but the accuracy of the latter is by no means certain. The fact that here, at Hesket-in-the-Forest, we are told that the burial was covered by large stones which were in turn covered by smaller ones, and that details of the burial itself are described, must mean that the burial itself had been deposited below the ground level as it was in 1822. Unfortunately, we have no means of knowing how that related to ground level a thousand years or so earlier.

The removal of the stones revealed a layer of charcoal, bones and ashes about fourteen feet in diameter. It is clear that both this layer and the fact, noted at the time of discovery and reinforced by recent inspection, that some of the objects found had 'passed through considerable heat' imply the presence at or near the site of a fire. The fact that no skeleton was found might further be thought to imply that the burial was a cremation. Against this we must note the presence of unburnt objects and the presence, below the layer of charcoal and ash, of a layer of fine sand. Such sand is often acid, and bones do disappear in acid soils.

The grave goods included some of the same items as at Aspatria. There was, for instance, a sword, though apparently unlike that from Aspatria (if Rooke really saw it rather than drew it from a description) this one had been bent, with its tip further bent, thus rendering

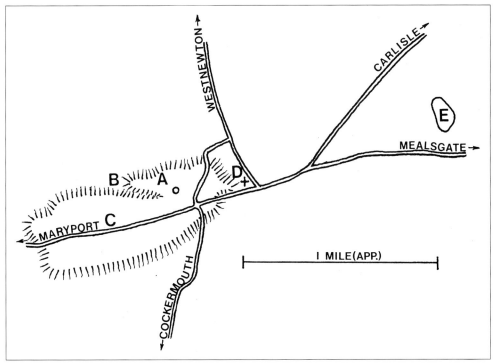

Figure 2. Sketch map of part of Brayton-with-Aspatria. The highest ground (over c.250′ above sea level) is hachured. A = the site of Beacon Hill; B = the 'hidden' dry valley; C = in this area is ground as high as Beacon Hill; D = the parish church; E = Brayton Park Lake.

it useless (a process sometimes described as 'ritual killing'). The guard of the sword had a ring-chain pattern inlaid in silver. It was this pattern which indicated most clearly that some of the items had been in fire, for its condition, as evident today as when it was described in 1832 ('silver, which has melted, but still adheres to [the guard and the pommel] in globules') was almost certainly caused by heat. Suggestions that the cause might have been misguided attempts at conservation seem to be rendered impossible by the contemporary observation already quoted. The sword had been broken by the time an assessment of Viking burials in Cumbria was made in 1934 (Cowen 1934) and its tip had been lost. One is forced to imagine that here a misguided attempt had really been made, this time to straighten it.

In addition to the sword, Hesket-in-the-Forest also yielded, as at Aspatria, a horse bit and an axe head. As far as can be seen from the Aspatria illustrations, the two were very similar, although the Hesket bit was said to have once been bronze-plated. Other items from Hesket related to horse riding and replicated at Aspatria were a pair of spurs. By the time of the 1934 search already alluded to, these had been replaced by a later medieval pair, but their shape is clearly depicted in the contemporary illustration of the 1822 find. Almost everything else found at Hesket has survived, though there are one or two small problems about the illustration, as will be seen. This survival is in happy contrast to the situation at Aspatria, whence all the finds are now lost.

Where the Aspatria find produced the exotic gold buckle and strap-end, Hesket yielded only two small iron buckles, one with part of its attachment to its strap, but other items were more widely represented. There were, for example two iron spearheads, one of them with a decorated socket. Both of these had been somewhat bent, but neither sufficiently to suggest that the damage was deliberate. There was also a shield-boss,

whose presence presumably indicates that of the shield itself, though nothing was noted of any other part of the shield. Aspatria was said to have had 'traces' of a shield.

All of the finds so far described fit reasonably well with a concept of the person buried at Hesket as an aristocratic, horse-riding, weapon-wielding warrior. This is less true of the remaining finds – an iron sickle blade, a whetstone and a bone comb and its case. The sickle blade was small and curved, with a bent tang to fit into its handle; the whetstone a simple rectangular-sectioned piece of stone without other surviving features. The comb was one of the type made by rivetting a number of small flat plates of bone side by side between two long pieces. Once that process had been completed, the teeth were cut and decoration applied to both sides of the handle (See figure 3). In this particular case, the illustration of the one surviving portion of the teeth shows that decoration had been applied to that also. The comb itself, or rather its teeth, were then fitted between two further long pieces of bone rivetted together to form a case or guard. All this assemblage was in as many as eight portions when found.

We have so far described twenty one pieces from Hesket, if all the eight portions of the comb just mentioned were really parts of it. It is just possible that two of them were parts of some other object, but if so, they were not mentioned in the text. Whatever the truth of that, the twenty one objects form Plate II of the volume of *Archaeologia Aeliana* in which they were described. Plate I occurs somewhat earlier in the volume, and because illustrations were far more sparse in such publications over 150 years ago, not all the items on Plate I relate to Hesket at all. Figure 1 is a Roman altar from Castlesteads; figure 2 is a plan showing the road deviating round the cairn prior to the destruction of the latter. The plan also marks 'Count Thorn and Seat' – the reference being to a tree marking the meeting place of the Manor Court of Inglewood Forest Nether Ward. There is still a thorn tree at this site and a nearby house has perpetuated the name of Court Thorn. Given its size, the present tree is presumably a successor of that marked on the plan on Plate I. Both the direction 'To Penrith' on the plan and the accompanying text tell us that the cairn lay to the east of the road, and therefore presumably somewhere near the site of the present house.

It will be recalled that the plan was numbered Figure 2. Figures 3, 4a, 4b and 4c are described in the text as a stone with two holes and a groove, a piece of a sandstone quern, a piece of a lava quern and a possible sandstone quern. The caption to the plan however, says 'All the Antiquities excepting the Stones were found here'. We cannot, therefore, say what, if any, connection the pieces of stone had with the cairn, or exactly where they were found.

We have not yet quite finished with the problems of Plate I. Figure 5 is a drawing, in two halves, of a view of a mound or cairn. It has no caption, but the mound appears to be surrounded with large stones, seventeen in number, of which three are labelled A, B

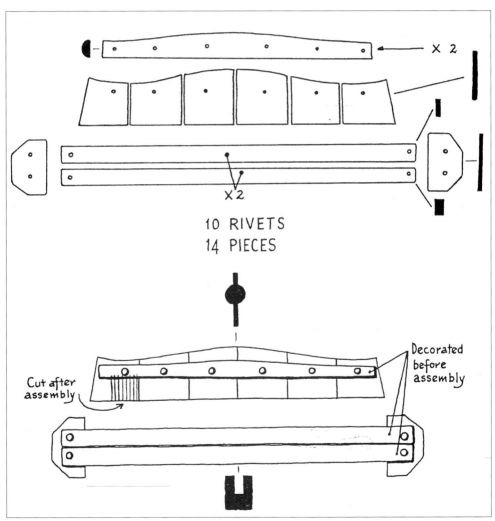

Figure 3. Method of construction of a bone comb and case like that from the Hesket burial.

and C. The whole thing is presumably a view of what the cairn looked like prior to its destruction by stone quarrying.

There are always problems in dealing with early accounts of archaeological discoveries, and doubtless our successors will find some of our accounts of modern work less than satisfactory. When we turn to another piece of roadwork which was proceeding further south in our area a little later in the year 1822, most of the problems lie in the interpretation of what was found, rather than in working out the meaning of the contemporary account. It is true that the difficulties of understanding the discoveries made at Claughton, near Garstang, were increased because careless copying in later versions of the account of the find introduced unnecessary obscurities, but it is possible to rectify this (Edwards 1970).

Let us look first at what was actually found. The building of a new road was initiated in this case by a desire to remove it further from the vicinity of Claughton Hall. In constructing the new road, the builders removed a small mound of sand. That they bothered to do this, rather than building the road a few feet further east or west suggests that the mound was fairly insignificant. Within the mound was found the remains of some sort of wooden structure and a group of grave goods. Here, of course, we encounter the problems caused by the lack of an exact account of the discovery itself rather than of the finds. We have no means of knowing what was the relationship between the wooden structure and the other finds, or between the various finds. The word group, used above, suggests that they were all closely related, but they may have been dispersed in some way through the mound.

Individually, the finds are not difficult to understand, and almost all of them either survive today or are shown in good contemporary illustrations. The single exception was a pot, containing cremated bones. This, as nearly always in early discoveries, was broken

by the workmen and lost. The frequency of this occurrence is caused, of course, by the natural desire to see whether or not the pot contained anything of value. In addition to the pot there were a small stone axe-hammer and seven items of metalwork. The latter were; of iron, a sword, a spearhead, an axe-head and a hammer head; of bronze, two oval ('tortoise') brooches; and of silver, a small brooch which had been converted to that use from an earlier function.

The implications of these finds are interesting and partly uncertain. A mound containing a pot with a cremation and an axe-hammer suggests a Bronze Age tumulus. As support for this view we can say that Bronze Age cremations in urns set in mounds are frequent, while Viking age cremation is not certainly attested in this country, though it might be thought that the Hesket burial, described above, tends to suggest cremation, though not buried in a pot. However, as we shall see, there is a hint of another Viking burial accompanied by a pot not far from Claughton.

Further support for a Bronze Age date for the mound comes from the fact that the stone axe-hammer is undoubtedly of that period. Such implements are, however, seldom deposited with burials.

The other side of the argument is equally possible to support. The presence of the wooden structure would not suggest the Bronze Age, while Viking burials in wooden chambers are known. It seems improbable that if Vikings wished to use an existing mound in which to insert their burial, they would dig far enough into it to insert a wooden chamber. The labour would be almost as great as that of constructing a new mound. The axe-hammer seems to be less of a problem, particularly as it is a very small and neat example. Among the Viking pantheon, the god Thor was symbolised by his hammer, and many amulets depicting this are known. It is not difficult to imagine a Viking coming across a small stone axe-hammer, collecting it and treasuring it as the symbol of the god, and finally being buried with it. In the absence of further evidence, which is unlikely to be forthcoming, we shall never know the truth for certain.

Compared with the question of the date of the mound, the Viking artefacts themselves are fairly straightforward. The first thing which should be emphasised is that they represent in some sense a double burial. The four iron objects all pertain to a male and the oval brooches to a female. Behind that simple statement, however, there are some complexities. The oval brooches were found back to back, 'forming a kind of box', they contained two beads and a molar tooth, and the whole was almost certainly wrapped in cloth. This is not what we might expect if the brooches had been buried with the body of the lady to whom they belonged. On the other hand, it is entirely understandable if they were buried in some way in token of her presence.

This might have meant as some kind of memento if she had been buried elsewhere, or it is perfectly possible to imagine their being buried with a cremation. No bones were recorded as having been seen at Claughton, so one could suggest that the male was also buried as a cremation accompanied by unburnt tokens of his earthly existence. We have, however, already remarked on the possible disappearance of bone in sandy, acidic soil, and the Claughton mound was specifically said to have been of sand. Perhaps the more likely scenario is of the interment of the male figure accompanied by his tools and weapons, his amulet and his memento of his wife. Let us remember the two odd beads (one red, one blue) and the molar tooth which were enclosed between the oval brooches. Does this not sound like a keepsake? And if such an interpretation seems to conjure up the figure of an unexpectedly sentimental Viking, then perhaps we are getting a little nearer to remembering that the subjects of archaeology were people like ourselves, variable in character and behaviour. All that said, we have still not squared the circle, for the pot and its cremation are unaccounted for.

The Claughton finds were made on the land of the Fitzherbert-Brockholes family of Claughton Hall, and the surviving ones (quite probably all of them at one time) were preserved there for many years. This ownership by a member of the landed class is important because it almost certainly accounts for the fact that drawings of the finds were made and accounts of them were written by two local antiquaries who were members of that same class. The first of these was John Weld of Leagram Hall, near Chipping.

Surviving watercolours by Weld (1813–1888) are almost all of architectural subjects (including Claughton Hall), but he painted the brooches and beads from Claughton at an unspecified date. He also wrote a clear, if slightly ungrammatical account of the find which became the basis, unacknowledged, of several printed accounts. He apparently owned illustrations of the axe head and hammer head, and, possibly, of the sword and spear head.

The second illustrator of the Claughton finds was Edward Jones. His watercolours of all the then preserved elements of the find belong to the Society of Antiquaries of London, but between them, the Weld and Jones illustrations raise a problem in the case of the sword and spear. The latter were exhibited to the Society of Antiquaries in 1846 by Michael Jones, brother of Edward, and a summary of the account was published.

The Jones brothers were members of a local family, and were related to the Fitzherbert-Brockholes of Claughton, their paternal grandmother, before marrying their grandfather, having been married to John Brockholes of Claughton; that grandmother's sister had married John Brockholes's son, William.

To return now to John Weld; the illustration he possessed of the axe head and the hammer head was a monochrome version of that of Edward Jones.[3] That is to say the point of view is the same, the shadows fall in the same way, and so forth. He may have painted it himself from Jones's painting or Jones may have painted it for Weld. In the matter of the sword and spear head however, the case is less simple. Jones's painting and the engraving based on it show a sword with a down-curved guard and a spear head with a raised mould-ing running round the socket. Each is accept-able as a Viking weapon. Weld, on the other hand, had a sketch of a sword with a straight guard (and incidentally lacking part of the hand grip) and a spear without a moulding. These are not captioned as being from Claughton, but where else could Weld have seen such things in 1834, the date of the paint-ing? Again, tantalisingly, we may never know, but the suspicion exists that the 1834 painting shows what was found at Claughton as they looked twelve years later, while the 1846 illus-trations show what was thought to have been found as far as it could be deduced another twelve years later.

It is good that though the iron objects have all disappeared, the three brooches and the two beads have survived to the present day in the family of the owners of Claughton Hall.

The two oval brooches (figure 4) are of Jansson's type P51 (Jansson 1985), 'the most common of all oval brooches', in which the tortoise-shaped gilt bronze shell which covers the safety-pin-like working parts was itself covered by a second shell pierced and engrav-ed with a decorative, originally animal-based, pattern. This would have been rivetted to the lower shell with the result that light, passing through the piercings of the upper shell would have reflected from the gilt surface of the lower shell, thereby causing the brooch to appear to sparkle. There were also four settings joined by saltire-shaped channels in which would have been twisted silver wires. These settings and wires do not survive. Brooches of this kind were produced by the hundred in Scandinavia, doubtless by work-aday craftsmen rather than artists, but, worn in pairs, one on each shoulder, to secure a

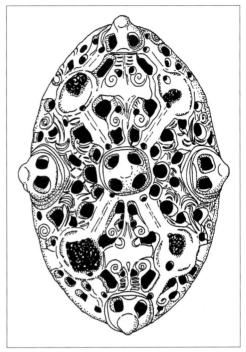

Figure 4. The outer shell of one of the two oval broaches from the Claughton burial. Length 3⅞″ (9.7 cm)

lady's pinafore-like outer garment, they must have provided an element of barbaric splen-dour.

The silver 'brooch' (figure 5) is another example of those pieces of metalwork from Carolingian Europe which have already been referred to. As found, it had had a small projection pierced with a hole rivetted to one end, and this presumably functioned as some sort of fitting. Originally, though, it had been one of a group of pieces decorated *en suite* which elaborated a baldric – a sword belt. How such things came into the possession of Norsemen in the west of Britain cannot be known. There is an instant tendency to think in terms of loot, but this should probably be resisted. Items of metalwork which can be shown to have been made in Britain and Ireland and which ended up in Scandinavia probably have a good case to make for their having been acquired by force. European ma-terial in Britain, while it may have been taken

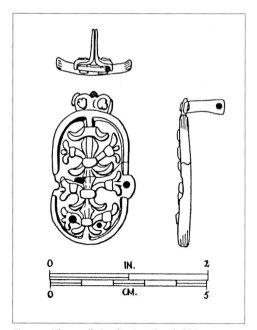

Figure 5. The small Carolingian silver baldric mount, later converted into a brooch, from the Claughton burial.

from its original owner, may equally have made its way west by way of trade.[4]

The three Viking burials we have so far considered have a number of things in common, and we shall come across some of these characteristics in discussing some of the cases where a discovery was probably that of a Viking burial, but the evidence is less than conclusive. For example, all three burials were covered by some sort of mound or cairn. That is to say that they were externally marked. They contained grave gods which consisted mostly of weapons and tools and decorative items. There is no hint in them of Christianity, which ought, if it were a factor, to eliminate grave goods, and therefore to make Viking burials undetectable and undateable. Less clear factors common to two of the three burials include hints of re-use of prehistoric sites and suggestions of cremation, or at least of the use of fire.

It has long been accepted, however, that the discovery of objects of Viking type or date

in churchyards could be taken as evidence of contemporary burials. Sometimes such objects were merely isolated objects, and their force as evidence of burials is comparatively slight. In other cases there was clear evidence of a burial within a churchyard, which prompts questions about the date and status of the churchyard and of the person buried there with accompanying grave goods.

Such a burial was found in 1898 in Ormside churchyard (Ferguson 1899). The cause, not surprisingly, was the digging of a grave for use at that time, and consequently it was not possible to follow up the discovery. Within the modern grave were found a skeleton with a shield boss and a piece of channel-shaped bronze which looks suitable for the binding of the edge of a shield. There was also a small knife and a sword. The similarity of contents to those from, for example, Aspatria will be obvious, and one wonders what else might have been found had it been possible to explore further. The answer might well have been nothing, because the one thing one can say with certainty about a churchyard is that it has been frequently disturbed. Had the sort of mundane iron objects found in any of the graves so far mentioned turned up in the past in Ormside churchyard, they would have excited little comment and almost certainly no record. But something else had turned up in the past at least 75 years earlier, and because it was not iron and not mundane it had excited considerable interest. This object was the Ormside Bowl, and will be described later (p. 39–41). For the point of view of our present concern with burials it is unfortunate that we know nothing of where within the churchyard it was found, so we cannot say whether or not it was related to the 1898 find. The Ormside Bowl is not a Viking object in origin, but its presence at Ormside is usually attributed to the Vikings, and the simplest explanation is that it came from an earlier disturbance of the same Viking grave as that dug into in 1898. Otherwise, unless we can explain its presence without involving the Norsemen, we shall have to imagine at least two Viking burials within the churchyard.

Another point about the known Ormside burial concerns the shield boss (figure 6). Our evidence for the date of the earliest Norse arrival in the area we are dealing with is slight and concerns largely the southern end of the region. Without that evidence there is little to go on. The sum total of the archaeological evidence is not great, and what there is, as we have seen, is hedged about with uncertainties. We must, therefore, not make too much of the fact, but it remains true that, in isolation, the Ormside shield boss would be dated in the ninth century rather than the tenth. Even if the dating is correct, it is necessary to think about what it means. The use of datable grave goods for dating the graves in which they occur is notoriously unreliable. Even if one excludes occurrences such as those of Roman coins in Anglo-Saxon graves, there are possible factors at work to falsify the sorts of conclusions one might draw. For example, of course, the objects put into a grave may just be old at the time of their deposition. They, and this might be thought to be particularly true of warrior equipment, might have been owned by the dead man for most of his life. They may be even older if they had been handed down to him from a previous generation. They may be old and out of date so that they were considered suitable only for burying. There is no lack of instances of objects buried with the dead

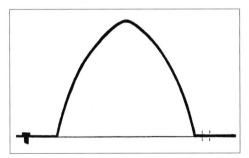

Figure 6. J.D. Cowen's sectional drawing of the Ormside shield boss (from Cowen 1934).

being in some way substitutes for what they represent. So, one shield boss is not going to redate the arrival of Norsemen in north west England. But it is a hint to remember.

Whatever *caveats* have been cited in looking at the four burials so far described, there is no real doubt that they represent what they purport to be – the last resting place of people of Scandinavian descent placed in the ground probably not long after the first Norse arrivals in the area. They are few, but that is not surprising. There were probably few Norsemen at first, and many factors will have been at work over the last thousand years to destroy their burials without attention being drawn to them or to keep them hidden for future generations to discover. But these four sites, two in the old county of Cumberland and one each in Westmorland and Lancashire, are not alone. There are twice as many sites where records tell us of discoveries which seem to fit our criteria, but where the evidence falls short of certainty.

For instance, there is the story told us by the Rev. John Whitaker, who published a work in the late eighteenth century misleadingly titled *The History of Manchester* (Whitaker 1775, 36–37). Misleading the title was because Whitaker's canvas was considerably wider than Manchester alone. He describes, in dealing with Blackrod, which lies to the west of Bolton and a good 15 miles north west of the city of Whitaker's title, a bit of folklore and what seemed to him to be physical evidence to support it. Before he wrote there had been inhabitants of Blackrod who claimed that it was the site of one of the battles fought by King Arthur, and they were able to quote the name of the commander in the battle in support of their contention. Unfortunately, by Whitaker's time, these men were dead and the crucial name forgotten. The alleged site of the battle had not been forgotten, however, and had been marked until about the year 1770 by a very large cairn. This had been destroyed, but had consisted of a 'vast collection of small stones from the bed of the Douglas'. It was presumably this river which had led to the folktale which Whitaker had been told, for two of the 'Twelve Battles of Arthur' had allegedly been fought on a river of that name.

When the Hasty Knoll, for such was its name, was removed, there were found 'fragments of iron'. These Whitaker considered to be 'the remains of those military weapons which the British reposited with their heroes at their death', for he naturally considered the mound to have been a burial place of the ancient Britons. We must pay him the courtesy of allowing that he knew the difference between iron and other metals, and if so, admit that the most likely period for the inclusion of iron weapons in a cairn in our area is that with which we are dealing.

Under the mound Whitaker describes what he felt to be a grave, and it is difficult not to agree with him. He called it 'a cavity in the hungry gravel immediately under the stones, that was about seven feet in length; the evident grave of the British officer, and all filled with the loose and blackish earth of his perished remains.' Again one notes the lack of bones, and wonders if the 'blackish earth' implies ashes. If the general uncertainty of evidence from a site such as this, seen and described over two centuries ago, tempts one to fly rash kites, it might be pointed out that the derivation of the word hasty, in its normal modern sense, actually relates more to ideas such as turmoil, strife, than to speed.

Our knowledge of the next burial to be considered is an example of what can be achieved by a museum curator armed with knowledge of his collections, perseverance, and a modicum of luck. All these were required to identify (Cowen 1948b, 1967) a sword of which the broken remains were in the collections of the Society of Antiquaries of Newcastle upon Tyne. Once its labels had been collated with those in an early catalogue and its provenance narrowed to Eaglesfield, in Cumberland, an account of the sword was published. This, in turn, led to information coming to light about its discovery in 1814 on a hill called Endlay or Tendley, together with a skeleton and two other metal items now lost. The first of these was called a halberd in the contemporary description and the other a fibula. The halberd was said to have been eleven inches in length, and seems likely to have been a spearhead. Since it, like the sword, which had inlaid silver decoration on its guard, was described as much rusted, it, too, was probably of iron. The 'fibula' was stated to have been of bronze, and its pin was five inches in length. The description of the ring at the top of this pin suggests that that the object was a ring-headed pin not unlike that from Brigham (p. 20), but the precise details of the description of the decoration of that pin led the author of the modern publication to compare it with an elaborate ring-headed pin from Norway. There were apparently other burials on the same hill-top, but they seem to have been later in date. In this they resemble those found on the hill of Flusco Pike near Penrith whereon also a great Viking penannular brooch was found.

Another site having some similarities to that at Blackrod is Brockhall Eases, Billington (Raines 1849, 286). This lies in the valley of that river Calder which has flowed through Burnley and Whalley, not far from its junction with the Ribble. The strange-sounding name derives, apparently, from the Old Norse *ey*, meaning formally an island, but occurs fairly often as the name of a flat area nearly enclosed by a loop or meander of a river. In this it used in the same way as the Old Norse *holmr*, meaning sometimes an island and sometimes a near-island.

Here, at Billington, the farmer, Thomas Hubbersty, removed a large earthen mound in 1836. In it he found what is described as a 'Kist-vaen' of rude stones, that is to say a chest- or box-like structure. This contained some large human bones and a number of iron spearheads which 'crumbled to dust on exposure to the air'. As in the case of Blackrod, we have to assume that the contemporary description means what it says and, bearing in mind the burials already described, admit that this sounds like a Norse burial.

Whether or not our next piece of evidence is considered sufficient to indicate the former presence of a Norse burial depends on the acceptance of the opinion attributed rather vaguely to 'Norwegian scholars' some years ago (Cowen 1948a, 74). This was to the effect that any Norse object found in a churchyard can be taken as evidence of a burial. If this is disregarded the evidence is indeed slight, consisting only of a bronze ring-headed pin (CW$_2$4 (1904), 340). It was found in the course of underpinning the foundations of the tower of the church of St Bridget at Brigham in Cumbria. Now, of course it is possible for a Viking object to get into the ground in a variety of ways, of which deposition with a burial is only one. That a church was later built on the site might seem to add weight to the supposition, and the further fact that the church contains Norse sculpture might yet further support it. It must be said, however, that the very presence of Norse sculpture in a church proves that Norsemen have been in the immediate vicinity, and where more probable to lose a cloak pin than near the door to a building? If it be objected that pin and sculpture are of different dates one must still bear in mind that a church containing sculpture earlier in date than any surviving portion of the building might well have been preceded by a yet earlier church contemporary with the pin. In all, it has to be felt that a single item of everyday jewellery found in a churchyard is no more than possible evidence of the former presence of a furnished burial.

We are on somewhat firmer ground, though not without uncertainties, when we come to consider the finds made at Crossmoor, Inskip, in the Fylde of Lancashire in 1889 (Fishwick 1891, 2–3). The immediate occasion of the discovery was gravel digging, and thus the recorded depth of ten feet is somewhat suspect. That is not to say that the

gravel excavation was not ten feet deep, but that untrained reporters would not necessarily have distinguished between the depth of the excavation itself and the precise depth in the ground at which the objects lay. These were three in number, a sword, a 'dagger' and a pottery vessel. Sword and 'dagger' were preserved at the time, though not, of course, the pot. The 'dagger' (?spearhead), of which no description seems to exist, has subsequently disappeared, but the sword (figure 7) is still available to be examined. It is of a Norse type in which the top of the grip is concave, to accommodate, presumably, a pommel of organic material (wood, bone, horn), while the guard turns downward.

The real rarity in this particular discovery was, of course, the pot. The contemporary description says that it had 'evidently been a cinerary urn', but does not state clearly in what way this was evident. It may be that it contained cremated bones, but in that case it might have been expected that the account would have said so. On the other hand it may be that it was 'evidently' a cinerary urn because complete pots found in the ground usually are. The description of the vessel is fairly precise, but not sufficiently so to bring to mind any known type of vessel. It reads thus: 'It was of extremely rude workmanship, and the heat to which it had been subjected had left it almost black ... The shape of the urn was round, narrowing from the base and then broadening out, and again contracting at the mouth; the rim of the mouth was slightly ornamented with curved lines'. This suggests some kind of globular vessel with a foot, but its black colour and the decoration on the rim do not fit readily with any likely candidate.

What are we to make of this? There are hints of cremation at Hesket, as we have seen, but the site which most closely parallels Inskip is the closest geographically, Claughton. The pottery vessel found there has usually been dismissed as Bronze Age because of the presence of the stone axe-hammer. Perhaps

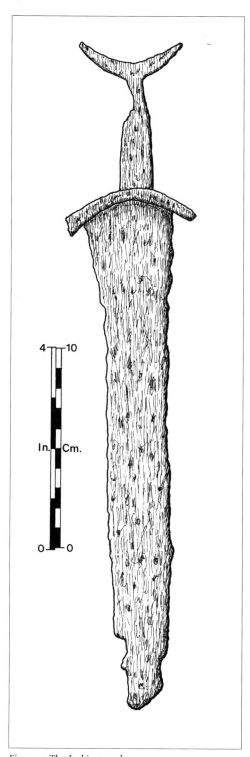

Figure 7. The Inskip sword.

the occurrence, within five miles of each other, of two sites at which undoubted Viking objects were found associated with pottery vessels perhaps containing cremations is significant. There is, at any rate, enough evidence to enable us to say this: there is no inherent improbability in Viking cremations; our total sample of what was probably always a fairly small number of furnished Viking graves in our area is very small. Let us not ignore perfectly good evidence on the basis that it conflicts with received ideas, but bear it in mind to weigh against any further discoveries. 'Not proven' is the verdict at the moment, but the case cannot be totally thrown out.

Our remaining possible burials are three in number, and all depend on the discovery of swords. One of these bore evidence which suggested that it might have come from a burial, another came from a churchyard, thereby gaining in probability. The third has no such credentials, and is included here only on the basis that all the eight other swords from the area seem to have at least some evidence to associate them with burials.

The first of these was found at West Seaton in Cumbria (CW_24(1904)335) in the winter of 1902–3 in a gravel bank variously described as being 67 yards south-east of West Seaton Vicarage or 80 yards north of the river Derwent. The sword had been bent, which has been taken to mean 'ceremonially bent ... and therefore ... from a grave'. The overall length of the sword was 80cm (31½″) of which some 8cm (3¼″) were accounted for by the grip. The description of the find seems to suggest that the sword was still in its scabbard. It has unfortunately been lost.

The churchyard find was made at Rampside, to the south-east of Barrow in Furness (Gaythorpe 1910). The cause of the discovery was, as at Ormside in 1898, the digging of a grave, but the area in which the grave was dug had been disturbed relatively recently, either by the construction of a wall of the Sunday School in 1842 or by its destruction in 1892, possibly both. This disturbance meant that there was no likelihood of finding any details of the burial, but the sword which was found, partly within the modern grave, was of some interest. The pommel, grip, guard and 40cm (1′ 4″) of the blade survived, and displayed the peculiarity that it was apparently single-edged.[5] Bearing in mind that the find was made in 1909, the attempts to wrest some more information from the fragments make modern-sounding reading. The word fragments is used with good reason, for it was small scraps of the blade, found outside the area of the modern grave which were submitted to two different authorities for investigation. First a fragment was sent to Miss Rayner of the Botanical Department of University College, Reading, who confirmed what must have been suspected – that the rusted fragment showed traces of iron-impregnated wood fibres suggesting that it had had a wooden scabbard. Unfortunately, she was unable to identify the species of wood involved.

For the other expert witness, recourse was had to home-based skills. If there was one thing the Naval Construction Works at Barrow in Furness knew about, it was steel, and so the report of Mr Weekes of that institution was comprehensive, including analyses of both metal and corrosion products. He was able to say that 'analysis … proves conclusively that the sword was made from … "steely iron" – or wrought iron containing carbon', and that 'the material was not made by one of the modern processes, and … it was … delivered from the furnace … in the form of semi-fused globules agglomerated together, that were subsequently welded by hammering in this form'.

This brings us to our last trace of a possible burial, a sword found allegedly eight feet down in a bed of gravel at the foot of Whitbarrow Scar in Witherslack, Cumbria (Hutton 1901). It is possible to suggest a likely find-spot for this sword given the statement about a bed of gravel and the further

comment that the site was continually flooded in winter. After its discovery some time in the nineteenth century, the sword was kept at Witherslack Hall. It subsequently went missing for a time, but is now in Kendal Museum.

Such, then, is the totality of our surviving evidence for Viking burials in our area. At first glance it may not seem to amount to much. Closer consideration suggests that it may be quite significant as an element in our knowledge of Norse settlers in north west England. We have, first, quite a bit of direct evidence about burial customs. Recurring elements of weaponry and horse gear are themselves suggestive of the beliefs of those buried, and the existence of forms of cairn or burial mound tells us something about the desire to keep alive something of the memory of the dead. Conversely, we may note the lack of any evidence that any attempt was made to record who was buried in a particular spot.

Another interesting point which begins to emerge is the evidence for widespread cultural contacts. The continental gold buckle and strap end from Aspatria and the silver baldric fitting from Claughton are the beginnings of evidence for contact with the mainland of Europe, not necessarily direct, but which is not in the least surprising and which we shall see reinforced when we come to consider objects which might be considered as loot and others connected with coin hoards.

The final aspect of the evidence from graves which is worth emphasising is the light they throw on the living. We can deduce where people lived in north west England during the Viking period only from other kinds of evidence, direct traces of settlement being almost entirely lacking. Burials are likely to have occurred not too far from settlement sites. Anthropological studies have shown that sometimes burial is carried out by rule or custom away from settlement; the best known ancient parallel is the Roman prohibition on burial within settlements. Such burial is, however, rarely at great distance and it is much more likely that burial sites give some general indication of settlement sites. Although it is true that the total number of burials, even when the possibles are included, is a very small sample on which to base any thoughts, it is interesting that to plot these twelve sites (figure 8) gives a distribution not greatly different from that produced, first by adding the hogback tombstones discussed in the chapter on sculpture, and secondly by adding all other finds (figure 9) of Viking material.

Incidentally, it should perhaps be pointed out that theoretically most of the burials referred to, since they included grave goods, were pagan burials, or at least burials following pagan rites. It is presumably implicit that

some at least of the sculpture found associated with church sites was memorial in character, and that therefore burial in Christian Norse or Norse-oriented societies took place in or around a church. This simple view has to be modified by other facts. First, the association of early churches in Scandinavia with pre-Christian monuments. It is with this in mind that such statements about Viking artifacts found in churchyards as that quoted for the Brigham pin make sense. Such a pin may have been associated with a pre-Christian burial on the site which later became a churchyard; it may simply have been incorporated in a burial in its utilitarian purpose of retaining whatever textile (clothes or shroud) was included with the burial. The

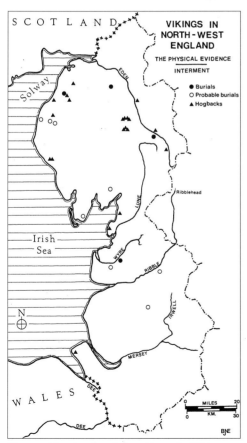

Figure 8. Map showing all the evidence for Viking age burial in north west England.

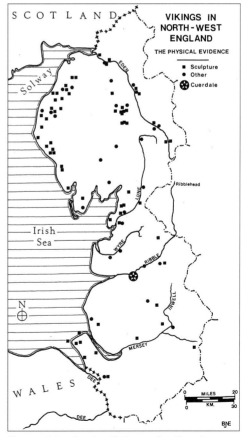

Figure 9. Map showing all classes of artifactual evidence for Viking age activity in north west England.

third possibility is the most interesting – that it was included in a burial because of lingering pagan habits. That this might have been the case is hinted at by the statement made that when the Heysham hogback, surely a Christian monument, (see below, p. 95) was first disturbed, a sword and a spear were found accompanying the skeleton. We have seen that both these types of object are of regular occurrence with pagan burials, and we have here an example of just what we might expect. On the whole, death-bed reversions are probably more common than death-bed conversions; and funerals are conducted by the living survivors, who may or may not respect the wishes of the dead.

Notes

1. Rooke, of Mansfield Woodhouse, Nottinghamshire, had sent an account of some antiquities in Cumberland and Westmorland to the Bishop of Carlisle, who was Vice-President of the Society of Antiquaries of London, and this had been printed in *Archaeologia*, vol. IX, for 1789. The following volume, for 1790, contained two papers by Rooke, in the first of which, 'Druidical and other British remains in Cumberland', the Aspatria burial is described. By 1790, Rooke was a Fellow of the Society. One wonders whether he was related to John Rooke, of Aikton (1780–1856), the economist. Aikton is about 10½ miles (*c.* 17km) north east of Aspatria.

2. Something very like flowers is by no means impossible. A well-known sword from Ballinderry Crannog I, Co. Westmeath, has engraved decoration on its guard looking much like flowers, which may well have been inlaid.

3. Well reproduced in Richards 1991, colour plate 10.

4. In connection with the converted Carolingian mount, it is worth quoting the words of Johs. Boe of Bergen Museum, writing in 1932 about an Anglo-Saxon bronze mount found in Norwegian grave. He wrote (Boc 1932, 442): 'Besides the two tortoise brooches a third brooch was generally carried, placed in front of the dress ... Rather common were Celtic bronze mountings or *other objects of foreign origin furnished with a pin and adopted* [sic] *as brooches*' (my italics).

5. Single-edged Viking swords are known. Several were among the swords excavated at Kilmainham, near Dublin, in the nineteenth century.

CHAPTER THREE

Weapons, jewellery, loot

We have already observed that discoveries of Viking settlement sites are less likely to be made than, for example, those of burials, because the remains left are unlikely to attract the attention of someone who knows nothing about them. The other side of that particular coin is represented by most of the items to be dealt with in this chapter. People's attention has always been caught by such objects as weapons found in the ground, and any kind of jewellery is usually noticed.

We are not, of course, here going to deal with any swords, because practically all the Viking swords found in the area have some evidence to suggest that they were associated with burials. Small knives or daggers, which we have noted being discovered in burial deposits along with swords, do not attract nearly so much attention, and none which seems likely to be of Norse origin or type seems to have been recorded as a casual find. The next most obvious weapon used by the Norse was the spear, and at least five spear heads have been found in our area. All are of some interest either because of details of their manufacture or their find-spot, or both.

The earliest of these discoveries was as recent as 1942, when a spearhead was unearthed during operations to recover a material called 'diatomite' in Kentmere (Fell 1956). This was a water-laid deposit containing the skeletons of the microscopic plants called diatoms. They are better known for their occurrence in chalk, where they are marine in origin, but freshwater species also exist, and the material containing their chalky skeletons was in demand as part of the war effort in 1942.

This first spearhead found in Kentmere (figure 10b) was 13½″ in length and had grooves round the socket which once presumably contained decorative silver wires. Its socket, unlike that of most Viking spearheads, was split, which led to the suggestion that it might have been an Anglo-Saxon copy of a Viking type. Given the geographical location of the find, and the discovery of another Viking spearhead in Kentmere, this seems unlikely. The second spearhead (figure 10a) is longer than the first and has a much more complex socket. This has quite an elaborate moulding at the blade end together with three pairs of grooves nearer the shaft end. Between these pairs of grooves are the remains of two rivet holes some 5mm in diameter.

Work by Mr John Anstee of the Museum of Lakeland Life and Industry (pers. comm.) has shown that the first spearhead has two areas of pattern welding (figure 11b) running from near the base to about half way along the blade. From here to the tip a central weld is marked by a slight keel. Mr Anstee suggests that each pattern weld consists of a short 'rope' of three iron strips twisted anti-clockwise.

In contrast, the second spearhead (figure 11a) carries evidence of 'pseudo-pattern welding' in the form of twisted iron pieces forged into recesses punched on both sides of the blade. While the blade is welded to the socket in each case, the second spearhead does not have a central weld.

The third spearhead found in our area was recovered in 1976 from the bed of Esthwaite Water (Unpub.) (figure 10c). It lies midway in length between the two Kentmere examples and has two pairs of grooves round the socket at each end and in the middle – a

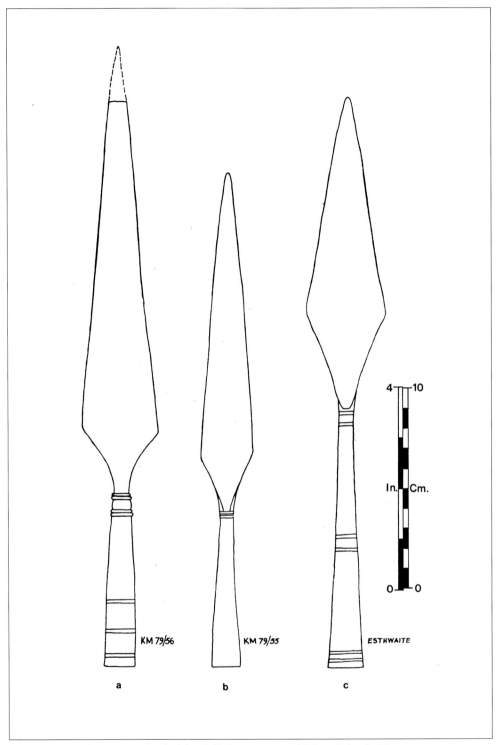

Figure 10. Three Viking age spearheads: (a) and (b) from Kentmere; (c) from Esthwaite Water.

total of twelve grooves. It still retained part
of its wooden shaft when found.

What are we to make of three spearheads,
two found in water laid deposits and the
third actually in water? The practice of deposition of weapons, principally swords, in
water is well known from the Bronze Age,
the Iron Age and the later medieval period.
Is there here a hint of the continuation of
the habit in the Viking period, but involving
spears?

For what it is worth, we have two more
spears to consider which do not appear to be
associated with water at all. The first was
found during excavations for extensions to
the factory of Storey Brothers of Lancaster in
1961 (*Med.Archaeol.* 6–7 (1962–3) 308) (figure
12). Although no archaeological investigation
took place so we cannot be certain, no other
objects seem to have been found. It is true
that had any other oddments been present
they might well have been ignored, for this
is an astonishing weapon. It is very nearly
two feet long, and was bent when found. It
is no small tribute to its maker that it was
straightened and the only evidence of the
process to be seen today is a slight irregularity
in the line of the blade. It, too, contained part
of its wooden shaft within the socket, which
might suggest that the deposit in which it was
found was waterlogged. Its find-spot to the
south of the City of Lancaster and the lack
of expert witnesses to its discovery make
speculation as to the reason for its presence
both inevitable and profitless.

The two Kentmere spearheads are in Kendal Museum and the Esthwaite Water and
Lancaster spearheads in Lancaster Museum.

Our final spearhead is a less spectacular
weapon, 21 inches (53.3 cm) long, found on
the Nan Bield Pass in the Lake District
(Unpub.). However it came to be there, it
had not been sacrificed or otherwise deposited in water! The Nan Bield Pass,
incidentally, leads out of Kentmere.

All the items so far discussed in this chapter have been weapons. We now come to

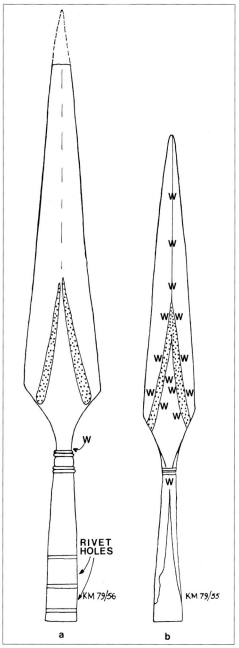

Figure 11. The two Kentmere spears, showing
manufacturing methods, as deduced by J. Anstee.
In (a) the stippled areas represent 'pseudo pattern
welding, forged into punched recesses on both sides'.
In (b) they represent 'pattern welding; two ropes of
iron strips (probably three in each case) were twisted
up anti-clockwise and exist through the thickness of
the blade'. W = welds.

consider an item associated with a weapon, but not actually so itself. This is a chape; that is to say that it is the decorative piece of metal at the base of a scabbard which performs the dual function of protecting its lower end and of elaborating the scabbard. Although chapes are known from almost as long ago as swords themselves, these objects are not particularly common. It was pointed out fifty years ago, in discussing a chape from a site in Norway (Grieg 1947), that although quite literally thousands of Viking age swords are known, only a few dozen chapes of that period are recorded. Relatively little, of course, tends to be known about scabbards as opposed to swords. They were usually made of organic materials, thus being vulnerable to deterioration, were seldom highly decorated, and had nothing of the *cachet* and interest of the sword itself.

Given this background, the discovery in 1994 of a Viking period chape at Chatburn in the Ribble valley was somewhat surprising (Edwards forthcoming in *Med.Archaeol*). Indeed, only one other Viking period chape was known from the British Isles. This was found at York, in circumstances not closely recorded, in the early years of the century (Waterman 1959, 72). With the lack of readily available parallels to consider, the Scandinavian material had to be followed up, and this led to the first very interesting observation that the Chatburn chape was exactly paralleled by one excavated in 1937 at Gjermundbu, some 40km. north-west of Oslo. At the time of that excavation, it seemed clear that there were three main types of Viking age chape. Firstly, there was a type in which the decoration consists of a single ribbon-bodied creature with a head, a number of legs and a tail. It was not really possible to narrow the origins of the creature more closely, except to say that it had reptilian and mammalian overtones, rather then, say, avian or piscine ones. This beast had its head, seen from above, in plan, as the highest point of the chape, and the remainder of its body and limbs disposed in

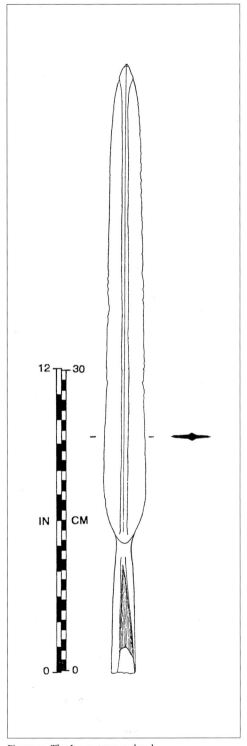

Figure 12. The Lancaster spearhead.

an asymmetrical way over the remainder of the chape. This type of chape was represented by that from York, together with Scandinavian and other examples.

The second type, represented by that found at Gjermundbu and by our Chatburn example (figure 13), had a decorative scheme based on two quadrupeds with their bodies crossing each other. The animals, though made fantastic in detail, were more realistic than the single beast of the York chape; they were clearly mammals and they clearly had a feature projecting from the head which much resembled a pair of long recurved horns. The general impression given was that the creatures were fairly closely based on something like an ibex. It must be admitted instantly that attempts to make this kind of identification are much frowned on by specialists in Dark Age animal art, who prefer to see the 'horns' of the Chatburn creatures as a 'head-lappet'! To be fair to all, it must be said that the resemblance, in the case we are considering, to an actual species of animal is closer than is often the case.

The excavator of the Gjermundbu grave described only one other type of Viking age chape, in which the decoration consists of a bird shown in the manner known to heralds as 'an eagle displayed' – that is as the German eagle is always shown. In the case of these chapes, the degree of distortion from nature is somewhat less than in the first two types. No such chape is recorded from Britain, though the nearest Continental example of a

Viking chape (from a ship burial on the Ile de Groix, off Brittany) is of this type.

Later research has shown that there are about 250 Viking period chapes known from all over Europe, and the author of the standard work on the chapes (Paulsen 1953) has divided them into seven classes of which only two concern us – Class I, decorated with birds, and Class II, decorated with animals. In Class II are a Scandinavian Group, which includes the York chape, and a Swedish Group, which includes the chape from Gjermundbu, and, therefore, our Chatburn chape. Paulsen lists 49 Class I chapes and 45 in Class II. It is clear from his distribution maps that their centre of gravity, and therefore probably of manufacture, lies on the island of Gotland. Figure 14 is adapted from Paulsen's maps and shows the distribution of the 29 chapes of the Groups including those from York and Chatburn. It will be seen that more than half the examples recorded lie inside a circle of 250 miles radius centred on Gotland, and that the distribution of both types extends from the Volga basin to western Europe (Britain and Iceland).

If the spearheads, discussed earlier, particularly that from Lancaster, are the type of object which is unlikely to be overlooked once unearthed, the remaining objects to be dealt with in this chapter are even more likely to attract attention. We have to consider first a number of silver brooches and then two or three other precious and/or highly decorative objects.

The word brooch in modern parlance usually applies to a decorative, sometimes highly valuable, piece of jewellery, often worn attached to a garment and often held in position by a version of the safety pin principle. Brooches in the past, before the widespread use of the button and buttonhole, were much more functional and correspondingly important. They could, of course, also be highly decorative, sometimes valuable, and apparently also might have other functions such as the denoting of status. An attempt is sometimes made to differentiate these functional

Figure 13. The Chatburn chape.

objects of the past from their less useful successors by the use of some such term as *fibula* for the ancient examples, but there is really no justification for this. In fact, all the Viking-period brooches we have to deal with in this chapter are of the type called penannular.

Since *an(n)ulus* is Latin for a ring, and the prefix 'pen-' (from *paene* or *pene*) may be translated 'almost', the distinctive feature of a penannular brooch is a ring with a gap. On the ring runs a pin, longer than the diameter of the ring, with a loop at its head. The pin is prevented from coming off the ring by a thickening of the ends of the gap in the ring. These thickenings are referred to as 'terminals', and provide the most obvious, though not the sole, place for elaborate decoration. In use, the pin is passed through the gap between the terminals, through the material of the garment to which it is to be attached,

and out again. One of the terminals is then passed below the protruding lower end of the pin and the ring rotated. The brooch is then firmly in place.

Since the part of the pin with a loop running on the ring of the brooch is obviously to be called the head, the opposite end has been referred to as the lower end. Nevertheless, there is evidence to suggest that in wear the pin of such brooches ran *upwards*, with the 'head' at the bottom. Ethnographic and legal evidence combine with common sense in the case of very large examples to make this probable.

The first two of these broches were found at different dates far in the past, but the second to be found, which has survived in the collections of the Society of Antiquaries of London, makes the understanding of the first easier.

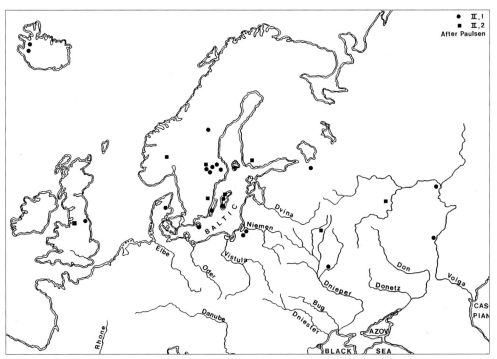

Figure 14. Map showing the distribution of Viking age chapes of the two types represented by those from York (Class II, 1 = ●) and Chatburn (Class II, 2 = ■) (Extracted from data in Paulsen 1953). A circle of 250 miles radius centred on the island of Gotland covers more than half the sites marked. It is 875 miles in a straight line from Gotland to Chatburn and the distance from Gotland to the sites in Iceland is 1400 miles and to that on the Volga 1150 miles.

The Antiquaries' brooch (figure 15) was found in 1847 'in a crevice of the limestone rock on the north side of Orton Scar ... not far from the summit, by a labouring man there employed in quarrying gateposts' (Birley 1964). In fact he found two objects, and we will return to the other in a moment.

The brooch consisted of a penannular ring with flattened and expanded terminals. These terminals carried engraved decoration. The details of this were shown by being left untouched, the background being shaded with parallel lines in various directions. First element among the design was a cross not unlike St Andrew's cross, but one of the arms was curved. This cross defined four zones which contained further decoration. The lines of the cross itself were originally covered with triple beaded wires, and these were held in place by domed rivets each with a beaded wire collar. There were, of course, five of these rivets, one in the centre of the cross and one at each end of the arms. Each of the four zones defined by the cross contained a contorted fantastic creature with a bird-like head, ribbon body and three legs and feet. No two of these eight creatures (on two terminals) were alike.

The pin of this brooch was looped round the ring, and the loop held in position by a rivet. The head of the pin carried punched decoration, and this means almost certainly that the pin was a replacement. Ordinarily, the pin would be fitted to the ring before one of the terminals, and thus could not be readily removed or replaced.

It has taken some time to describe this brooch, though a glance at figure 15 will make the situation much clearer. The type is, however, a well known one, called, very reasonably, the Bossed Penannular Brooch. This label covers a variety of sub-groups, but the distribution suggests that they were almost certainly made in Ireland. How far they thus qualify as Viking artifacts is a matter of argument, but they were certainly in use in a Norse *milieu*, and the punched decoration

Figure 15. The Orton Scar brooch: detail of the terminals. Width of ring 4⅞" (12.5 cm). (By courtesy of the Society of Antiquaries of London)

on the replacement pin of this particular example is specifically Norse.

If further confirmation of the Norse context of this particular brooch were needed, the object accompanying it would supply it. This was a silver object called, for convenience, a torque, which is, strictly speaking, a neck ring. This particular example is, however, about 5½" in diameter, which makes it rather small for a neck and rather large for an arm. If we assume – though it is not necessarily true – that the brooch was the property of a lady, then the small neck size is less of a problem. The torque was made by twisting a bar of silver, and its terminals, which allow it to be put on and removed, consist of a pair of hooks in planes at right angles to each other. The springiness of the silver allows them to be moved relative to each other to make or open the fastening.

As has been said, the Orton Scar brooch is of a well known type and is still in existence because both Orton objects came into the possession of a Kendal antiquary called Thomas Reveley, who presented them to the Society of Antiquaries of London.

At the end of the eighteenth century, however, no such knowledge of Viking antiquities was generally available. Indeed, the Orton finds were thought to be Roman when they were first mentioned in print. In view of that kind of uncertainty, it is perhaps surprising that the earlier discovery of parts of a brooch of the same type as that found at Orton was recorded at all. The recorder was Thomas Pennant. He is probably best known for his contributions to natural history, having published an important work on zoology and been one of Gilbert White's correspondents for the *Natural History of Selborne*. Pennant, who came from Flintshire, also published descriptions of a number of journeys which he carried out, and one of these was his *Tour in Scotland ... of 1772* (Pennant 1790). In order to get from Wales to Scotland he had to pass, among other areas, through Cumberland, staying, as was his wont, with members of the landed classes. At one such overnight halt, Brayton Park, not far from Aspatria, his host told him of a discovery made when the park fishpond had recently been deepened. Two objects which Pennant described were a piece of decorated silver and a silver hook. Had they, or particularly the decorated piece, been described only in words their nature might still have been obscure. Pennant, however, travelled with an illustrator, one Moses Griffith, who later produced the illustrations for the plates in Pennant's books. Though he did not completely understand the decoration of the piece of silver found at Brayton, there is no doubt from his illustration that it was part of the ring and one terminal of a brooch very similar to that from Orton, and we may reasonably deduce that the silver hook was the pin of the brooch bent in two. Unfortunately, despite rumours to the contrary, these pieces do not seem to have survived.[1]

Another silver brooch was found in a field near Casterton Hall in the nineteenth century and eventually passed into the collections at Tullie House Museum, Carlisle (Cowen 1934, 184) (figure 16). This is an interesting brooch because of its relative simplicity, both in construction and decoration. It consists of the ring of the brooch with one of its two terminals and the head of the pin with a stump of its shaft. The terminal is globular with a slightly expanded cylindrical projection, and the head of the pin is of more or less the

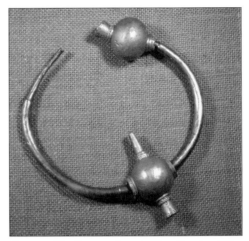

Figure 16. The Casterton brooch. Ring diameter 5¾" (14.6 cm). (By courtesy of Tullie House Museum, Carlisle)

same shape, the pin apparently passing through the globe. The shape of the two parts of terminal and pin-head are not dissimilar to that of a thistle flower, where the globular portion is green and the projection normally purple. What we have here, then, is a simple version of the thistle brooch at some more elaborate versions of which we shall shortly be looking. In the case of this Casterton example, the missing terminal shows clearly how the ring was tapered to allow it to be fitted over, and that, unlike the case of the bossed brooches represented at Orton and Brayton, the terminal was made separately. The rear of the surviving terminal of the Casterton brooch, like the rear of the pin head, is flattened and both bear crude decoration poorly executed with a simple punch and a compass.

It has perhaps been implied that there is nothing out of the ordinary in the size of any of the brooches we have so far considered, and that is a little misleading. The pin of the Orton brooch is over eleven inches long, and the rings of the three brooches between four and six inches in diameter. By comparison with modern decorative brooches these are certainly large, and may well be thought of as perhaps a little inconvenient in use, even given that they were probably pinned to thick woollen fabrics.

The size of these brooches, however, pales into insignificance when we come to look at the next two, where the pins are both over one foot eight inches in length and the rings a little under eight inches in diameter. These two brooches, which are now in the British Museum, came from the neighbourhood of Penrith (figure 17), and are the largest of their type known in complete or near complete condition. The details of their discovery are tantalisingly slight, the first having been found in 1785 on a hill now called Flusco Pike to the west of Penrith (*Gent's.Mag.* 1785, I, 347), and the other in 1830 with its find-spot recorded only as 'near Penrith' (Cowen 1934, 183). It has been suggested that they may have come from the same deposit, but they are not an exact pair, and the chances are that we shall never know.

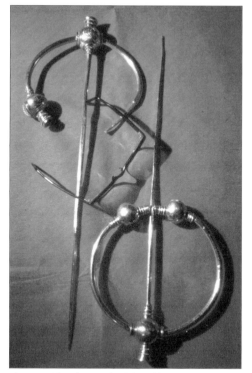

Figure 17. The Flusco Pike (r.) and 'near Penrith' (l.) brooches, with spectacles for scale. (By courtesy of the British Museum).

Parts of Fluskew (then so spelt) Pike had been enclosed in the late eighteenth century, and from 1773 finds had been made in the course of ploughing the enclosures. These included evidence of burials, some in stone coffins, but no suggestion was made that the brooch found in 1785 was in any way associated with these. Its sheer size made it instantly well known, and it was the historian of Northumberland, Durham and Cumberland, William Hutchinson, who immediately brought it to the attention of the learned world in the *Gentleman's Magazine* (1785: I, 347). It is true that he did not advertise his part in this, the note being subscribed with the letters W. H. to one side and B. C. to the other. It is these which make it certain that W. H. was Hutchinson and less elusive than Shakespeare's Mr W. H., for B. C. is Barnard Castle, the historian's home for the last fifty or more years of his life.

If the Lancaster spearhead was, as has been suggested, an astonishing weapon, these two brooches from the Penrith area are even more astonishing, and it is very difficult to convey their sheer size and magnificence. The human eye tends to assume that any object whose general shape is familiar is of about the norm in size. Thus Mount Everest looks little more impressive in a photograph than Ben Nevis, and thus it is with these brooches. To see them 'in the flesh', and even more, to handle them, is instantly to be impressed. With the exception of one missing terminal from the 'Penrith' brooch (which was still present 30 years after its discovery – does it lurk in someone's collection somewhere in Cumbria ?) they look as good as the day they were made. And because they are large, the details of their manufacture are easier to see than in the case of smaller examples.

Let us deal first with the elements which they share, reserving discussion of differences. Both brooches, then, have plain circular section rings with the terminals added to tapered ends in the same manner as the Casterton brooch. The terminals and the pinheads are globular, though the terminals are somewhat flattened, and all carry on their front faces the form of decoration usually called 'brambling', thereby confusing the botanical metaphor. This was done by saw cuts, and the reverses of the terminals and heads show where the ends of these cuts were not totally controlled. Either side of terminals and pinheads are a number of collars, and the reverses are decorated. So, too, are the tops of the pin-heads.

The Fluskew Pike brooch of 1785 is slightly the simpler of the two. Two only of the three collars which surround the pin-head and flank the terminals are notched, the centre one being plain in each case. The top of the pin-head, its reverse face and the reverse faces of the terminals all bear compass-drawn decoration. An attempt has been made, with varying degrees of success, to produce five-petalled flowers in this way, and it seems strange that a craftsman who could produce such work as the brooch itself clearly did not understand the principles of making compass-drawn flowers.

On the 'Penrith' brooch, greater elaboration occurs. All three collars of pin-head and terminals are notched, and on the terminals, herringbone, zig-zag and Greek key patterns occupy the bands between them. The top of the pin, the reverse of the pin-head and the reverse of the one surviving terminal all have a pattern consisting of a ring of radial lines surrounding an area divided cross-wise, in each sector of which is engraved a triquetra, or three-pointed knot. In the case of the reverse of the pin-head, one quarter of the surrounding band becomes a kind of guilloche pattern. Finally, there are traces of decoration on the front of the pin itself for some four inches roughly between the terminals. It is interesting that the omission of 'brambling' on the reverse faces is clearly intended to obviate problems of snagging the material on which the brooch was worn, and that the wear on the decoration of the pin, sufficient to prevent the recovery of the pattern, must have been caused by use for some considerable period.

In the context of the dangers caused by the wearing of brooches with pins over a foot and a half in length, the following has been quoted from the Irish Brehon Laws of the ninth century (Dunraven 1874): 'Men are guiltless of pins upon their shoulders or upon their breast, provided they do not project too far beyond it; and if they should, the case is to be adjudged by the criminal law'. Without attempting to judge what might be meant by 'too far beyond', which sounds like the sort of phrase discussion of which results in lawyers growing fat, the importance of this quotation is that the subject was of enough concern to generate a reference in the Laws.

Passing reference has been made to a suggestion that both of the brooches from the Penrith area might have come from a single hoard. While this is probably beyond resolution, events in 1989 might be thought relevant. Part of Flusco Pike has retained the name Silver Field, presumably in recognition of the 1785 find. In this area was discovered in 1989 all or part of at least half a dozen more silver brooches (Unpub.).

It is worth pausing at this point to consider the types of brooches which we have been discussing in a wider context, before returning briefly to the recent find on Flusco Pike. In common with 'tortoise brooches', which are now known as 'oval brooches', some penannular brooches of the Viking period have received new nomenclature. What used to be known as 'thistle brooches' are now called, rather infelicitously, 'ball-type brooches', while bossed penannulars are classified into six groups (Johansen 1973). The re-naming of thistle brooches avoids any implication that their makers intended any part of them to look like thistles, just as 'oval brooches' disclaims any intention to refer to tortoises. The 'thistle' simile was always somewhat confused by the tendency to refer to the cross-cutting on their terminals as 'brambling'. Nonetheless, attempts such as these to introduce greater precision in such names are really unnecessary; if anyone is interested enough to want to know what a thistle brooch is, he will soon find out, and the name is merely convenient shorthand for use with other people who also know.

The 1989 Flusco Pike find consisted of the following: two ball-type ('thistle') brooches; two bossed penannulars more or less similar to that from Orton Scar, though one of these had an important difference from all similar brooches; and a bossed penannular of a different type. In addition, there were five fragments which could have come from either of the first two bossed penannulars, and a complete pin which is unlikely to have belonged to either. The blade of an axe found nearby, though its origin is indeterminate, is interestingly similar to one found with Scandinavian objects in York in 1902.

The two thistle brooches were both of moderate size and fairly simple when compared to the two great brooches found there in the past. The ring of one (figure 20) had been badly distorted and one terminal had been dislodged, but it was recovered. The pin of the other, (figure 18) which had lost its tip, was 10.4" (26.3cm) long.

The bossed penannular brooches consisted of a near-complete example of Johansen's Sub-group B (figure 19) and part of two Sub-group A brooches, The Sub-group B brooch is complete apart from the tip of its pin. It is the first of its class to be found in England, though there were fragments at Cuerdale, and this fact draws our attention to the number and distribution of these Hiberno-Norse penannular brooches. They are rare objects. The total numbers known are something of the order of 50 'ball-type' (including those represented by fragments) and 45+ bossed penannulars of all types, and the distribution of each is interestingly similar. They are fairly widespread in Ireland and there they are in greatest numbers. There are a few in Cumbria, Lancashire, Cheshire and Yorkshire, and a very few in Scotland and the Isles. In the

case of ball-type brooches, the numbers are somewhat unbalanced by a single find in Orkney, and there are a couple of Scandinavian finds of bossed penannulars. It will readily be understood from this that, though these splendid brooches are immediately associated in our minds with the Vikings, their homeland is not Scandinavia, and it is almost certain that they were manufactured under

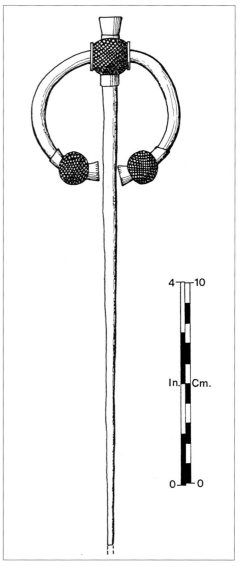

Figure 18. Ball-type ('thistle') brooch from Flusco Pike, 1989.

Norse influence in Ireland, or just possibly in north-west England.

To return to the examples of this type from Flusco in 1989, the five fragments found of a Sub-group A bossed penannular brooch came from a unique example of the type. Four of these fragments joined to form part of the ring and much of one terminal. The remaining fragment was a large part of the other terminal. Reconstruction of the decoration showed that, unlike any other brooch of this class, the fields of decoration each containing an animal were defined by ribbons which ran *from* the central boss and *bisected* the space between the bosses, rather than *joining* the bosses. This resulted in four bosses per terminal, and, of the eight bosses thus defined, six were recovered. In artistic terms, the importance of this differing mode of definition for the decorative fields lies in the fact that they are more nearly square or rectangular, and thus easier to fill.

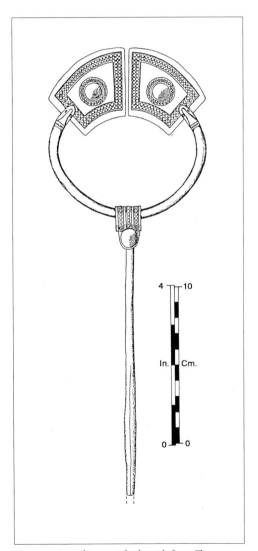

Figure 19. Bossed penannular brooch from Flusco Pike, 1989.

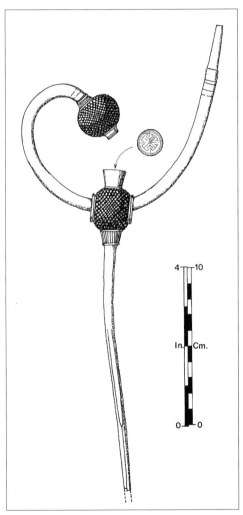

Figure 20. Damaged ball-type brooch from Flusco Pike, 1989. The ring of the brooch was damaged at or prior to discovery, and one terminal detached. This was, however, preserved.

The full publication of this find, whose contents were declared Treasure Trove at an inquest in Penrith, is awaited with great interest (Graham Campbell, forthcoming).

After consideration of such exotic objects as the great silver brooches from the Penrith area, it is almost an anti-climax to concern ourselves with what must have been a much more everyday form of garment fastening in Viking times. This is the ring-headed pin, and we have come across one such already in discussing the Eaglesfield burial (p. 19), albeit probably a rather elaborate example. As their name implies, ring-headed pins consist of two parts – a pin, usually a few inches long and bronze and a moveable ring attached to the head of the pin. They are not spectacular and seldom come to notice. The Eaglesfield pin was recorded, after a fashion, because it accompanied a burial. Another we know from Brigham churchyard, possibly with a burial. Others are recorded from our area, particularly a number from another place where they were unlikely to escape notice. That was the shore of the Wirral, in the vicinity of Meols (Hume 1863), where, over a number of years in the mid nineteenth century a vast quantity of material, mostly metal and of widely varying dates, was recovered. The significance of these Wirral finds has not been fully worked out, though some form of Viking trading place has been postulated as an explanation of some. The records of the finds are not all that might be desired, either, but nineteenth century publication and twentieth century study have shown that at least four, and probably up to a dozen such objects were found. More recently, another turned up in the vicinity of Arnside Tower.

Ring-headed pins were unspectacular workaday objects in the tenth century. One other small, but not quite so mundane object must claim our attention before we pass on to what might be classified as loot. This is a convex disc whose precise function is not clear. It may or may not have been a brooch, but its decorative scheme recalls some east Scandi-navian work, and, in particular, the type of pendant found in a burial near Saffron Walden in Essex (Evison 1969, figure 3a & b and pl. LXXI).

The object was found in the course of building operations at Castlefield, Manchester (Baines 1836, II, 159, pl. 3, no. xxiii; Bu'lock 1958, 113; Watkin 1883, 113), between 1828 and 1836. It was first considered to be Roman, but was identified as east Scandinavian with parallels at Hedeby and Birka in 1958. The actual description of the object seems to have baffled writers. The first to appear in print described it as 'inlaid with seven stones in a kind of mosaic work', which is apparently completely without foundation, as is a later statement that it was originally 'set with fictitious gems of paste, of which traces remain', More recently, it has been stated that 'earlier accounts suggest that it was once silver gilt with niello inlay'.

A recently recognised addition to the list of Viking adornment from Cumbria is an arm-ring (Graham Campbell 1995, 38), now in Tullie House Museum, Carlisle, which was found, apparently in the 1970s, on the shore of the Solway not far from Gretna, but within the English border. The parish is therefore, presumably, Kirkandrews-on-Eden. It was made by producing a tapering rod of circular cross-section. This, about 23cm in length, was then bent round into a circle of about 7cm diameter and the two ends twisted together to secure them, though one is now slightly damaged. Telling evidence that, although described as an arm-ring and here classified as jewellery, this piece was at some stage regarded solely as bullion, lies in the presence of a dozen nicks (see p. 62). The weight – just over 56 grams – is about one eighth of a pound.

Each of the three remaining objects included in this chapter was, so far as we know, found by itself. All are of some decorative worth and in no case have we a proper account of their finding. The chapter heading classifies them as loot, and what that means is that all three are exceptional items found at an unlikely place and that their date suggests that they might have reached that place as a result of the wide-ranging activities of Norse people. It must be emphasised that there is no certainty, and future research may shed a different light on any of them.

Perhaps the most obvious candidate for this classification in one way is a small bronze boss found at Ribchester.

The story of this piece is a mixture of good luck and bad luck. Its first mention in print was in 1883, when it formed the subject of an engraved tailpiece to the chapter on Ribchester in W. Thompson Watkin's *Roman Lancashire* (Watkin 1883,163). Watkin knew perfectly well that it was not Roman, but he clearly liked the look of it, and had a drawing and from it an engraving done. He does not specify the findspot beyond Ribchester, nor does he say when it was found, though we might legitimately guess that it was fairly recently or it would have been mentioned elsewhere in print.

Neither does Watkin tell us that the engraving was the actual size of the object. This we can deduce from the mention of the boss in the *Victoria County History* (Farrer and Brownbill, I: pl.f.260). Here it is illustrated by a rather poor photograph, but its size is given. This, incidentally, shows that it was not, as suggested, a shield boss. The function of a shield boss is to accommodate the user's fist, and the Ribchester boss is under three inches in diameter.

These deductions as to the decoration, from the engraving, and the size, from the VCH, are necessary because, sadly, the boss is no longer available to be studied. The words 'now lost' are all too familiar to those who study antiquities, but in this case we can attribute the situation to human beastliness rather than to human frailty, for the Ribchester boss found its way to Liverpool Museum, whence it disappeared in the bombing of 1941. For our present purpose we may note that its scheme of ornament makes its origin in Ire-

land highly probable and that its function was likely to be wholly decorative. Like many another piece of decorative metalwork, it was part of the decoration of a larger object. As to its place at Ribchester, obviously no certainty is possible, but the Ribble valley lay on the York-Dublin axis so forcefully pointed out by the Cuerdale Hoard (see Chapter 5) and the boss may simply have been lost there by a passing Norseman or it may even have accompanied the burial of such a man in the churchyard there. The combination of Ribchester's Anglo-Saxon name, the dedication of its church to St Wilfrid, and the presence within that church of at least two fragments of late pre-Conquest sculpture suggest that there would have been a church and churchyard within the abandoned Roman fort at the relevant time.

Visually very different, another small piece of decorative metalwork with an even vaguer findspot has attracted much more attention than the Ribchester boss. This is a tiny gilt bronze head, now in the British Museum, from 'Furness' (Henry 1940, 123, pl.49, e: Youngs 1989, no.135) (figure 21). That word should strictly apply only to the peninsula on which was later founded Furness Abbey and still later Barrow in Furness. The name is, however, loosely used for the whole of the area of North Lonsdale or Lancashire-north-of-Sands, including the Cartmel peninsula. The head itself, which is barely an inch and a half high, has prominent ears and eyebrows. The face is moustached and bearded and the eyes protrude. All the areas of hair have been gilded and there were probably stones, possibly precious, set in the eyes and in a depression on the top of the head. Like the Ribchester boss, its home may well have been in Ireland and its route to the west coast of England unfathomable. Unlike the boss, however, it found a secondary function after being removed from whatever it was that it decorated, for it has been filled with lead. This has been done so that there is a channel all round the back of the object, and it may be that it was some kind of weight. It may be worth pointing out, in connection with the Furness head, that it bears a close resemblance to the portrayal of St Mark in the eighth century Lichfield (St Chad) Gospels (figure 22).

Last of our candidates for discussion under the heading of loot is by far the most visually impressive, enigmatic and exotic. This time we can narrow its findspot more closely, for it came from Ormside churchyard at some date prior to 1823 (Ferguson 1899). At this date it was given to the Yorkshire Philosophical Society and it remains to this day in the Yorkshire Museum in York. The circumstances of its discovery are entirely unknown, and there is at least the possibility, alluded to in our chapter on burials, that it formed part of the furnishing of the grave whose contents were further disturbed in 1890.

The Ormside Cup or Bowl is the general title by which it is known, and the ambiguity already hints at the curious nature of the object. No aspect of the vessel, its size and shape, its manufacture, its subsequent treatment and its decoration, is without its unusual or unique features. Let us begin, then by describing it. It consists of a shallow bowl whose maximum diameter (at the rim) is about 5¼″. Its depth is only just over an inch and a quarter and its base is about 2¾″ in diameter.

The construction of the vessel is peculiar in that the exterior consists of a silver sheet bearing repoussé ornament, the reverse of which is hidden in the interior by a gilded copper or bronze lining. The interior of the base carries decoration, as does the exterior, and they echo each other in that each has or had five bosses, one in the centre and four surrounding it. These bosses were metal on the exterior, rivetted on and surrounded by a band of plaited wire surmounted by a band of twisted wire. It is on these bosses that the cup would rest, and the central boss had been damaged by this process. In the interior only one of the bosses retains its setting, which is of blue paste. The empty central setting is surrounded by sixteen small settings in only one of which were any remains, said to be of a pearl.

At some stage in its life the base plate had become badly worn and detached, and had been replaced and held in position by a very crude annular patch fixed by 21 rivets.

We can distinguish a number of elements in the decoration. First, and most striking, is

Figure 21. The 'Furness' head. Height 1⅝″ (3.9cm). (By courtesy of the British Museum)

Figure 22. St Mark, from the Lichfield (St Chad) Gospels, for comparison with the Furness head.

the repoussé decoration of the exterior. This is divided into four sections by four metal bosses, of which two remain. The bosses themselves are about half an inch in diameter, though with their setting the diameter approaches an inch. It may be worth quoting at this point the words of W. G. Collingwood, who spent four days in 1896 making three drawings of details of the Cup (Collingwood 1899). Of the bosses he says they are 'bound round with twisted wire, and surrounded with repoussé circles, one plain and the other ornamented wth what at first sight looks like a mere row of dots; but it is really alternate dot and line on a very tiny scale; much more delicate than the repoussé work of the base …'.

The decoration the bosses divide can be rapidly summarised. Each of the four panels contains a plant motif spreading from multiple stems which arise from a kind of cross between a plant pot and a tree bole. The stems in two panels carry buds and leaves and in the other two bunches of fruit. Each panel is inhabited by four beasts which are all, strictly speaking, chimaeras, none being certainly attributable to a known species, and some not certainly birds or mammals.

The decoration of the base is in two parts, exterior and interior. The former consists of a repoussé interlace cross, filling the space within the circular plate left by the five bosses. In the interior the opprtunity for similar treatment was not so obvious, there being a greater discrepancy between the large central boss wth its surround of smaller settings and the four smaller bosses (figure 23). In the event each space has been filled with rather formless knotwork executed in twisted wire soldered on. Neither the artistry nor the craftsmanship of this element seems to match some of the rest of the work on the Cup.

Finally, there is the rim of the Cup. Above the plant and animal decoration of the exterior runs a band of small bosses bordered above and below by twisted wire. Riveted imprecisely in the centre of each quadrant

is a gem in a rectangular setting. The rim itself has been bound with a split tube held in position by five metal clips. Much of this apparent addition has gone.

Description is one thing; interpretation is another. We can say without much doubt that the object was old when it reached Ormside churchyard. The wear and the crude repairs say as much. The basis of its design and the source of the repertory of its decoration are elusive. No really convincing parallel for either has been adduced, and in a recent study devoted particularly to the animals (Yapp 1990), it was concluded that the author was 'fairly confident that there are no animals, with one exception, and no plant scroll, like those of Ormside on any English artifact of any age'. He was therefore forced to suggest that 'the Cup is an isolated work of genius with neither close predecessors or successors'.

It is, therefore, perhaps not surprising that

Figure 23. Two illustrations of the Ormside cup by W. G. Collingwood. (From Collingwood, 1899).

the Cup has always sat, and still sits, awkwardly in the pages of studies where art history and archaeology meet. Collingwood, a century ago (Collingwood 1899), had no such doubts. He saw the basis of the imagery as Mediterranean and the craftsmanship as Anglian. He concluded his notes on the Cup with a memorable sentence which we will quote with a relish which does not necessarily imply total agreement. 'Orm [of Ormside] must have been a Viking ... I am tempted to fancy that the cup was Orm's loot from York, or some great Anglian church, and the the clumsy ruffian smashed it as he went clattering over the fells, and then tinkered it up for his drinking bouts, or gave it to the priest, for the good of his soul'.

To that we may perhaps add that it was a vessel, not, for example, a decorative boss. The direction of the plants and the animals shows as much. But if Orm, or anyone else, used it for a drinking bout, he must either have had access to a very potent liquor or to have refilled it frequently, for it would hold less than a quarter of a pint.

Notes

1. The Brayton bossed penannular brooch was 'communicated' to Thomas Pennant by 'Dr Brownrigg' – presumably William Brownrigg, M.D., F.R.S., of Whitehaven (1711–1800), physician and chemist, author of *The Art of Making Common Salt* (1748).

CHAPTER FOUR

Coin Hoards

One type of discovery of ancient material which always makes headlines today, though it did not always in the past, is that of hoards of coins. The word 'hoard' suggests both considerable numbers and the intention of the original owner to put the coins aside 'for a rainy day'. In practice, numismatists tend to regard any number of coins greater than one as a hoard, and the intentions of the original owners are rather taken for granted, though there may be other reasons than 'savings' for the temporary deposition of a group of coins.

Often, of course, other items found with the coins are at least as interesting as the coins themselves, be they other items of value or containers of greater or less distinction. But the great thing about coins, particularly, though not exclusively, from the point of view of the layman, is that they can be dated with some precision. This means, firstly, that an estimate can be made of the date of deposition of the group: it cannot be earlier than the date of issue of the latest coin; considerations of numbers and state of wear can add accuracy to the estimate. Secondly, this can give valuable information as to the date of objects found with the coins, including containers. Thirdly, the date and distribution of coin hoards can be used to deduce ideas about the security or otherwise of conditions in an area at a given time.

All of these points are illustrated by the coin groups which fall chronologically and geographically within our scope. There are a dozen of these, and it is approaching half a century since the discovery of the latest. They range from two uncertainly recorded coins from Manchester found in the mid-nineteenth century up to the staggering

Cuerdale Hoard of 1840, described in Chapter 5. They were accompanied variously with jewellery and ingots. Their containers include clay pots, chests and more exotic metal bowls. As might be expected, their discovery was always accidental, and the accuracy of recording of contents and circumstances suffers as a result.

Nonetheless, they form an interesting element in the archaeology of the Vikings in North West England, and they will be described here in the approximate order of their discovery.

Having already said that the casual nature of the discovery of coin hoards often means that precise information is lacking, and considering that the first find we will consider was made in the early seventeenth century, it is surprising that we have quite a lot of evidence about it (Edwards 1992, 52–54). The reason for this lies in the character of the man who, though not strictly the original discoverer, was the landowner and rapidly became the discoverer of most of the hoard.

He was William Blundell of Little Crosby, and he had two traits of great importance to us. First, he was a staunch Roman Catholic; and, secondly, he was a great writer-down of things, a characteristic which persisted later in his family.

The importance of the adherence of the Blundell family to the Old Faith lay in the fact that William Blundell saw that various of his co-religionists were denied burial in the churchyard of the parish church at Sefton. He therefore decided to do something to alleviate the distress this caused by providing a burial ground on his own land. The spot he chose was called the Harkirke, and it seems improbable that the name had nothing to do with the choice of location.

The name is usually taken to mean 'grey or hoary church', and is recorded as far back as the late thirteenth century; it recurs in sixteenth century deeds, and so was doubtless current in 1611, when Blundell made his decision to provide a burial ground for Roman Catholics. His method, apparently, was to take a piece of ground fenced already on two sides and to complete its enclosure by ditches on the remaining two sides.

This was done, and the first burial took place on Sunday 7th April, 1611. On the following morning William Blundell's cattle were being taken to a field near the burial place under the charge of a fourteen-year-old boy called Thomas Ryse. As he crossed the ditch defining the burial ground, Ryse found a number of coins in the newly-disturbed sandy soil. Having safely left the cattle to graze in their appointed field, he returned to Little Crosby Hall, Blundell's home, and we may reasonably assume that he did so at a gallop, for we know he showed the coins to some of his fellow servants and thus Blundell found them, discussing the find. Blundell took charge of the coins (no 'finders keepers' for Ryse) and demanded to be shown whence they came.

The search party (for this it became) consisted of Blundell, Ryse, Nicholas Blundell (William's son) and Edward Denton. Richard Blundell, William's brother, soon joined them, and they searched until dinner time. After dinner Blundell, his brother and son and Edward Denton took with them Blundell's wife and his mother. They found some more coins, but not as many as before, and Blundell's estimate of the total found was 'above fower schore' i.e. more than eighty.

Blundell then set about making a record of the coins, writing the account from which the above paragraphs are derived (in Lancashire Record Office, ref. DDBl (Acc. 6121)) and drawing an example of each different type of coin. There were initially twenty five

of these, but then Blundell looked more carefully and found that there were five more varieties of the coins bearing the name of Saint Peter and two more coins of other types which he had not noticed.

He had then drawn both faces of thirty five coins out of a total of more than eighty. It seems mildly improbable that if the total were not much more than this number, and he had gone through them specifically searching for examples of each type, that he would have missed the two quite different coins. The varieties of the Saint Peter coins are wholly understandable, for the differences are small, but it seems probable that he would have been more likely to miss the other two only if the total had been some bit greater than eighty.

By itself, the record so far quoted would be a valuable body of evidence for any coin hoard, and particularly notable for one found as early as 1611. It is not, however, alone, for Blundell transcribed it into a small notebook (figure 24), bound in parchment bearing music on its reverse, and a copper plate was engraved from his drawings from which prints were struck. It is said, but on what evidence is indiscoverable, that the plate was engraved in 1613.

All three pieces of evidence quoted still survive, but sadly the coins themselves do not. Writing towards the end of the seventeenth century, William Blundell's grandson said there were 'about 300' coins, but thirty years earlier he had estimated 'dyvers hundreds'. This vague figure is rendered suspect by the fact that he also refers to the copperplate (which therefore cannot be later than 1655) which shows thirty five coins, but says there were 'at least 20' different varieties of coin.

Doubt was possible at this fairly early date because the coins were already lost. Exactly how this occurred is not clear. It is said that the coins remained at Little Crosby Hall until 1642, when, in the uncertain circumstances of the Civil War, they were sent to the vicinity of Wrexham for safe keeping, but were never seen again!

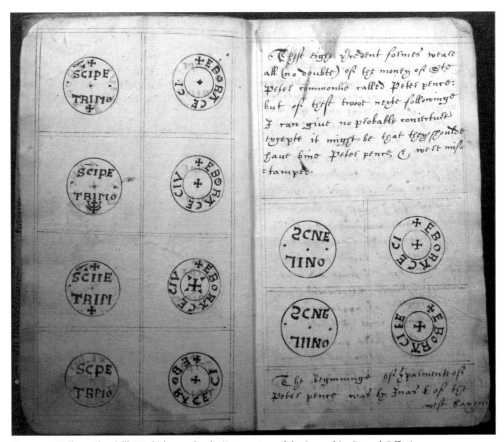

Figure 24. William Blundell's Harkirke notebook. (By courtesy of the Lancashire Record Office)

That this may just be a piece of anti-Welsh propaganda on someone's part is hinted at by two other accounts of the fate of at least part of the Harkirke silver. The first of these is the statement that there was, in the private chapel at Little Crosby Hall, a chalice made from the Harkirke silver, but this was stolen in the nineteenth century.

There is no corroboration of this story, but a second story which may in part be confused with the first, has good evidence to support it. There was, at the Roman Catholic church at Little Crosby, a pyx which had engraved on one side a Crucifixion and on the other the following inscription: 'This was made of / siluer found in/The burial place/W.Bl.' (figure 25). This object has been stolen within the last fifteen years, but photographic evidence

of its existence is preserved. Further, it was analysed by X-ray fluorescence in 1974 at the National Museum of Antiquities of Scotland. While no quantitative results of this analysis are known, the results were said to be consistent with the claim of the inscription.

What are we to make of this conflictng evidence? Let us grasp firmly at the pyx. Although now lost, both its appearance and something of its composition are known. Blundell recorded only coins from the site, and it is their fate which is detailed in the Wrexham story. The 1655 letter already referred to, although slightly suspect in matters of detail, does mention 'uncoyned silver', so there may have been ingots present as well. From here all is speculation, but it would have been entirely consistent with what we know of William Blundell had he kept an example of each of the coin types and arranged for any 'surplus' coins together with uninteresting-looking things like ingots to be turned to pious use in the manufacture of the pyx (?and the chalice). On the surviving evidence, a deposition date of about 910 is assigned to the Harkirke Hoard.

If the evidence from the Harkirke is surprisingly complete, particularly in view of the date of the discovery, that for the next hoard to be considered is tantalisingly vague. All that is known for certain is that 28 'Silver Saxon pennys' were found in Lancashire in 1734 (Blackburn and Pagan 1986,no.96). The record of this find is buried in the minutes of that remarkable body, the Spaldng Gentlemen's Society, as a result of the fact that drawings of the coins were exhibited to a meeting of the Society on 19 December, 1734. The minute records that the coins were like some illustrated in a volume called *Linguarum Veterum Septentriolanium Thesaurus … *by George Hickes (1705), and that variations between the newly discovered coins and those shown on Hickes's plate were

marked in red in the Society's copy of the book. There the trail almost ends, for the Spalding Gentlemen's Society's copy of the *Thesaurus* has disappeared.

However, less than a month later, the same drawings were 'communicated' to a meeting of the Peterborough Gentlemen's Society, and on this occasion the minute refers to a specific plate in Hickes's book. This plate illustrates 30 coins, some of which are types extremely unlikely to be found in Lancashire. Seven of the coins, however, are of the 'St Peter' type which we have already met in the Harkirke Hoard.

In the absence of further information it can only be guessed that the 1734 Lancashire hoard consisted of these coins, and that it was deposited *c.*AD 915.

We now come to our first hoard on which information was published at or near the time of its discovery. This was a group of coins found at Dean, 4 miles (7km) SW of Cockermouth and 6 miles (9.5km) SE of Workington, prior to 1790 (Blackburn and Pagan 1986, no.95: Strudwick 1958). A traveller, who preferred to hide under the cloak of 'A Lover of

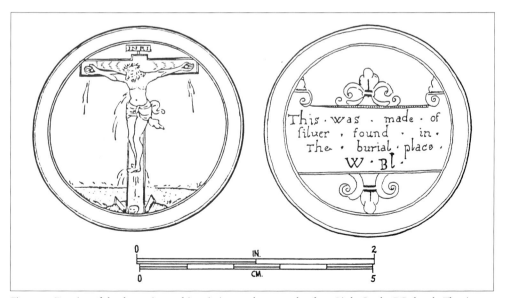

Figure 25. Drawing of the decoration and inscription on the pyx stolen from Little Crosby RC church. The ring was at the top, the hinge to the left of the Crucifixion side, and the catch at the bottom.

Antiquities', reported in the *Gentleman's Magazine* of August, 1790, that he had seen 31 coins from this hoard in the Museum run by Peter Crosthwaite at Keswick. He illustrated eight of the coins, from which it is possible to derive the exact identity of seven English coins and one from Italy. There were, apparently, three more coins of the same general type as these, 'marked with a cross'. In addition, the author illustrated one Arabic dihrem issued in the name of Al Muktafi-billah at the mint of Andaraba, some 80 miles (125km) north of Kabul in present-day Afghanistan (and, incidentally, one of the two remotest mints represented among the Cuerdale coins).

This last coin, he suggested, was typical of nineteen others from the hoard in Crosthwaite's Museum. An independent publication of oriental coins refers to four Arabic coins from the hoard, including one which must have been over a century old when the hoard was deposited, about AD 915. These four, and the one illustrated in the *Gentleman's Magazine* are presumably all part of the twenty to which the anonymous author referred. There seems to be no justification in attempts to add the numbers together. The hoard's composition, therefore, apart from any which Crosthwaite did not acquire, was 7 English, 1 Italian, 3 unknown, but apparently European, and twenty Arabic. The hoard, the finding of which resulted from 'a cow's treading upon the spot where it lay concealed' was in a leaden vessel, of which, unfortunately, we know no more.

We now move into the nineteenth century with the find made at Kirkoswald in 1808. Two near contemporary publications deal with this, albeit briefly. A third, which mentions the discovery, muddied the waters somewhat by a slightly careless footnote.

Let us try to sort certainty from probability. First, there were a large number of coins and a trefoil brooch set with garnets. That much is sure, though the earliest publication relating to these is the record, in the Donations List for 1814 of the Society of Antiquaries of Newcastle upon Tyne of the acquisition of 'Six Copper Stycas of the Northumbrian Kings, Eanred and Ethelred.' To this is appended the note 'They were found a few years since, near Kirkoswald, in Cumberland, by the blowing down of a large tree, the roots of which had taken hold of, and brought up with them, a large earthen vessel full of similar Coins'. This Donations List is sometimes bound with copies of the first volume of *Archaeologia Aeliana*, the Newcastle Society's journal, published in 1833. It is, however, separately paginated, and the Kirkoswald find is recorded on p. 3 of the List.

The description of the manner in which the find was revealed is circumstantial, and its plausibility is added to by the fact that, although the donor of the coins to the Society is listed as M. Atkinson, Esq., Carr Hill, Durham, the next donation listed was by Miss Atkinson of Kirkoswald, presumably a relative. Given these facts, David Wilson was surely right to suggest (Wilson 1964, 140) that the phrase used in Ruding's mention of the find in his *Annals of the British Coinage* (Ruding 1840, 233) – 'turned up by the plough' – was 'a conventional phrase of the period'.

Ruding gives the number of coins found as 542, which is generally accepted.

The carelessly expressed footnote occurs in a paper on a find of Anglo-Saxon coins from Hexham. Having described these coins, the author, J. Adamson, who was, incidentally, the Secretary of the Society of Antiquaries of Newcastle upon Tyne, mentions two other recent finds, that at Kirkoswald in 1808 and another at Heworth in 1813. His footnote says 'Ruding ... p. 223, Archaeologia Aeliana, vol. 1, p. 134' without making it clear that the reference to Ruding is for Kirkoswald while that to *Archaeologia Aeliana* is for Heworth. This has resulted in the Kirkoswald find having acquired the reference *Arch.Ael.*, 1, 134 on which page no mention of it will be found!

Interestingly, the hoard is given a deposition date (Thompson 1956, no. 225) of c. 865, before most writers would allow Norse incursions to north west England. By itself, of course, it means nothing, but it may be just another hint of disturbance prior to the opening of the tenth century.

We have seen good reason to think that the expression 'turned up by the plough' was a conventional one used in the nineteenth century of the discovery of items in the ground, and our last two hoards seem likely to have been exposed respectively by a cow and a wind. In the case of our next, however, there is every reason to believe that it really was a plough which caused the find. It was made in 1815 on land recently enclosed from Halton Moor (Combe 1815) in the Lune Valley under an act of 1797. There seems almost to be a deliberate attempt to keep the finder's name a secret. In one contemporary newspaper report he is called 'a farmer' and in another 'a freeholder of the manor'. Had we his name, of course, we could probably localise the find more precisely than somewhere in the 957 acres covered by the Act.

As a sample of the way in which such finds were reported in the early nineteenth century, it may be of interest to reproduce in full the text in the *Preston Chronicle* for 25 February, 1815.

Antiquities. – A farmer, whilst ploughing in the neighbourhood of Lancaster, lately discovered, a little below the surface of the ground, a silver vessel, containing about 860 small silver coins, and some other antiques. The coins are chiefly of the reign of *Canute the Great*, and may therefore be supposed to have lain in the earth about 800 years. There are a few which are evidently of an older date, and apparently of an inferior metal, having no legible inscription or mark, except a large cross on one side, and on the other a smaller cross, with the letter I on each side. The coins of *Canute* are in very good preservation, and the letters RE-ANG-CNUT, are very legible on one side, surrounding a rude figure, of a crowned head with a sceptre – on the reverse, the letters of the inscription, though very legible, do not appear to form any distinct words, nor has its meaning yet been made out. The vessel itself is of the shape of a common iron sauce-pan[!], widest near the bottom; the diameter at the top being 13¼", and at the widest part 15⅞", depth 8", and supposed content one quart, wine measure, its weight ten ounces; it was cased with lead, but is without lid, handle, or inscription; the sides are rudely engraved with uncouth figures of beasts and birds in compartments, and the intervals filled up with the representations of flowers and trees, surmounted round the top with an irregularly engraved border. It contained, besides the coins, small escutcheons or plates of gold, with a raised figure upon them, resembling a dolphin or fish of some kind; also a collar for the neck, made of silver wire, curiously twisted together, weighing 8 ounces, 6" in diameter, flattened at each extremity of the circle, and uniting by a rude sort of clasp. The land where these relics were found has been enclosed about three years.'

It should be noted that the dimensions given are wrong. As far as the two diameters are concerned, the figures are a pretty close approximation to the *circumferences* at those points. The depth, however, is totally wrong, being about four inches rather than eight. The weight given is not far wrong, but the capacity is little over half a pint. Perhaps the most interesting aspect of the paragraph is the statement that the bowl was 'cased in lead'. It will be remembered that the Dean hoard had a lead container, and others are known from other parts of the country.

There are four elements of the Halton find which require comment. These are: the coins; the gold foils; the silver torque; and, finally, the container.

The hoard was found on 12 February, 1815 and was sold within a few days to a Lancaster silversmith named Muncaster, who sent just under half the coins (400) together with two of the gold foils, the bowl and the torque to a Mr John Walker of Bedford Square, London. Through him they were exhibited at a meeting of the Society of Antiquaries of London, the account, by Taylor Combe, the Society's Director, being dated from the British Museum on 4 April and read on 6 April. 85 of the coins, one of the two foils, the bowl and the torque ultimately came into the hands of (Sir) A. W. Franks, and were bequeathed by him to the British Museum.

The whole of the 400 coins which went to London were identified, 21 being Danish and the remainder all of Cnut. No fewer than 366 of these were minted at York, only 13 being attributable to mints in the southern half of England. These were, with the number of coins appended: Lincoln, 4; London, 4; and one each from Cambridge, Chester, Exeter, Maldon and Winchester.

The remaining 460 coins were dispersed in the general vicinity of Lancaster. Records of the ownership of nine of these have been discovered by Mr Stephen Penney, all from the mint of York. Neither the identification nor the whereabouts of the remaining 451 coins is known.

The five gold foils which were not acquired by Sir A. W. Franks have also disappeared from sight, with one possible exception. The foils themselves are curious. They seem to have been created by impressing a thin gold disc over a die, of which the main element was loosely based on a helmeted head. At some later stage they seem to have been riveted onto some other object (figure 26).

All of the foregoing description is based on the surviving example in the British Museum, the engraving published by Taylor Coombe in 1815 and the absence of any note that there was any variation among them. One other item of information tends to support the use of the plural in the description above. Because the foils do not seem to be paralleled in Britain and because a statement was made in 1815 to the effect that similar foils were known in Denmark, information

was sought as to the presence of such things in the National Museum in Copenhagen. This showed that there is indeed one very similar object there, but it is as great an anomaly in Denmark as it is in Britain. Indeed, this single example in Copenhagen has been published in their catalogue of the curious objects called bracteates, with which it really shares little beyond being gold and being circular.

The important clue from our point of view, however, is that the foil in Copenhagen was not found in Denmark at all, but was bought by the Museum at Sotheby's in London in 1858, its only provenance being the collection of the Rev. T. F. Dymock. There is, of course, no certainty, but it seems extremely likely that the foil in Copenhagen is one of the missing five from Halton two of which were sent to London in 1815 (Edwards 1997).

The torque must have been, as Taylor Combe said, considerably compressed to get it into the bowl, and indeed shows traces of this and the reverse process today. That it suffered no more is testimony to the flexibility of this type of torque, made up of plaited

Figure 26. The small gold disc from Halton, now in the British Museum, and identical to that in the National Museum, Copenhagen.

wires merging into plate-like terminals provided with hooks, one in each plane. The terminals are further elaborated by twenty five impressions each of a triangular punch containing three pellets. The torque weighs just over six ounces.

The silver-gilt cup (figure 27) is an exotic object. Its size and shape are very similar to those of the cups from Fejø (Sweden), Pettstadt (Germany) and Ribe (Sweden), together with an unprovenanced cup in the British Museum. The decoration of the Halton cup is, however, unique, consisting of beasts and plant scrolls.

Below the rim, which is defined only by a small double moulding, is a running scroll which consists of a single stem meandering upwards and downwards. At the mid-level of each meander a tripartite leaf springs from a bound node, while two buds spring from the

Figure 27. The Halton silver-gilt cup, drawn by James Basire for *Archaeologia* in 1815.

stem between each pair of nodes. The stem runs anti-clockwise round the bowl and the leaves are thrown off backwards. An exactly similar scroll runs round the base of the vessel, except that this version runs clockwise.

Two further small mouldings separate the upper scroll from the main body of the decoration, which consists of four circular panels. These are two alternating pairs, containing, in the one case, a feline, and, in the other, a bovine creature. These vague expressions are used because it is not possible to be more precise about the species of animal depicted. The panels are separated from each other by four plant-based panels whose extremities develop into animal heads.

The feline panels show an animal running to the right, with its front legs extended before it and its hind legs behind it. It has small ears and a prominent eye and the open mouth reveals large teeth. The raised tail ends in quite a complex thickening or tuft. The feet are, however, apparently cloven. The animal runs in front of, and partly obscures, a plant-like growth which has four buds and two leaves visible above the animal. Springing to left and right so that they appear behind the animal's tail and in front of its chest respectively are two leaves of four and three divisions respectively, their presumed junction with the central stem obscured by the animal's body. Below the animal is a node with two three-lobed leaves splitting to left and right. The whole panel is surrounded by a double moulding with a continuous zig-zag line between the mouldings.

The bovine panel differs in several ways from that containing the feline, apart from the nature of the animal. The animal is stationary, left-facing and has its head lowered. Its hooves are clearly represented as such, complete with fetlocks, and its tail, raised in an S-shaped curve, has a tufted ending very similar to that of the feline. Left ear and eye are shown and the tongue is seen in the open mouth. A single horn only is shown, protruding from the animal's brow, a convention

proposed over half a century ago as one of the bases of the medieval unicorn (Bunt 1930).

Unlike the feline, the bull, which it must be, of whatever species, has below it a ground surface. This is depicted as a double wavy line producing three small humps. Between the lines are pellets and below the humps several rather vague wavy lines each ending in a small pellet. The only plant form in this roundel is a small thick stem with two bi-lobed leaves, in front of the bull. Both animals have rows of small tooled marks to represent hair.

The plant-form dividers between the roundels are again of two types. One is symmetrical above and below a central bound node. From this node arises and descends a central stem and a side stem to left and right. Passing up or down the central stem, it throws of to each side a bi-lobed leaf. Next it is joined by the tongues of the animal heads which terminate the side stems. Finally, the central stem ends in a lobe on each side followed by a tri-lobed finial. Each of the side stems throws off first a bi-lobed leaf on one side, then one on the other. Next comes a stem which is in fact a neck, since it has an animal head. These dog-like heads have pointed jaws and two sharply-pointed ears. Long tongues curl out of their mouths and rejoin the plant stem making the animal/vegetable transition in the same manner as the necks.

The other form of divider is asymmetrical about a horizontal axis (both are symmetrical about a vertical axis). There are two bound nodes on the central stem, and if we start at the lower of these and progress first upwards and then downwards, listing the projections on one side and remembering that they are repeated on the other, we get the following. Upwards: bi-lobed leaf; stem to which both animal tongues return opposite each other and ending in a bi-lobed leaf; node; bi-lobed leaf; stem splitting into bi-lobed leaf and animal neck; bi-lobed leaf. Downwards: bi-lobed leaf; bi-loded leaf opposite to animal neck; tri-lobed leaf. All stems and leaves throughout the decoration – vessel rim, plant forms in roundels, plant form roundel dividers, vessel base – have a central 'vein' shown.

The whole decorative programme of this vessel is alien, and as difficult to parallel as that of the Ormside Bowl. Its origin must lie in mainland Europe, possibly in an area where Carolingian and Italian influences mingled – perhaps not too far from the home of the Ormside Bowl itself.

Whatever the precise origin of these two highly decorative metal vessels, their presence in our area combines with that of foreign coins, both European and Arabic, and Carolingian jewellery, as in the Aspatria and Claughton burials, to indicate a society with far-flung connections, whatever the history of the individuals concerned.

Only twenty five years after the Halton find came that of Cuerdale, about which nothing further need be said here as it dealt with in the next chapter.

As far as we know the English coins in the Halton hoard consisted entirely of Cnut's 'Pointed Helmet' issue, so called because the king is shown wearing a helmet closely resembling those shown beng worn by the Normans in the Bayeux Tapestry. There were also a few coins issued in Normandy. Liverpool Museum has one coin of each of these two types which were given to the Museum in 1867 by Joseph Mayer. They are part of a wide-ranging collection of material listed in a catalogue, dated 1852, of Joseph Mayer's 'Egyptian Museum' in Liverpool and they are said to have come from Castle Hill, Manchester. No such location is known in Manchester, but the material apparently derived from the construction, across Castlefield, of the Altrincham to Manchester railway in 1849.

Six years later, in 1855, drainage work at Scotby, a couple of miles east of Carlisle, produced a group of up to 100 coins together with silver ingots and 'rods' (Blunt 1974:

Kruse 1986). Around 70 of the coins, all Anglo-Saxon, as opposed to Viking or foreign, and apparently the whole of the non-numismatic element of the hoard, have been traced. The latter consisted of six ingots or parts of ingots and four pieces of 'rods'. These are the first ingots we have come across, and it would be as well to describe them. There are a number of different types, but in general they are about the size and shape of small cigars. The comparison is useful in that there is some variation in size and shape of both. The single example from Scotby which is complete is about 2¾″ (7cm) long. Another, now broken, was over 2″ (5cm) in length.

Together with two 'rods', which are merely another way of handling silver bullion, the total weight of the non-coin element at Scotby was just over 210 grams – a little under half a pound of silver. It is interesting to note that this, one of three hoards from north-west England containing ingots, should have a deposit date of 935–940, lying between Cuerdale, c. 905, and Chester IV (below) of 965.

Mention of the Chester hoard of 1950, the latest find-date for any hoard dealt with in this chapter, brings us to the subject of hoards found in Chester, of which there have been four, here dealt with out of the overall date order of the rest of the chapter.

Of the first to be found, in Eastgate Street in 1857 (Blackburn and Pagan 1986, no.153), we know little. Up to 80 silver pennies were found, and a deposit date of 970 is suggested. Similarly, the St John's Church hoard (Blackburn and Pagan 1986, no.99) of five years later is ill documented. The number of coins was about forty and fifteen or sixteen were recovered, but cannot now be identified among the holdings of the Grosvenor Museum. The deposit date was about 917. The hoard of 122 pennies found near the north west medieval extension of the Roman fortress wall (Blackburn and Pagan 1986, no.174) is better recorded, and the deposition date is closer to that of the first to be found, about 980.

The final Chester hoard, and our last, is that rarity, a reasonably well recorded coin hoard (Webster 1953). Even here, despite the fact that the discovery was made close to the Grosvenor Museum, information was lost. Indeed it was nearly a fortnight before the Museum staff heard of the find, and, by dint of much hard work, recovered much of it. Their diligent work retrieved the container (a pot of considerable interest in its own right) and much of the contents, coins, ingots and hacksilver (see below, p. 63).

CHAPTER FIVE

The Cuerdale Hoard

The discovery of spectacular archaeological finds, whether accidentally, or as part of archaeological research, has the immediate and inevitable effect of unbalancing the previously held view of the area and period concerned. Sometimes, to the man in the street, the spectacular finds are completely distorting, so that, for example 'British prehistory' means 'Stonehenge', and 'Egyptian archaeology' is 'pyramids' or 'Tutankhamen'. When the find is treasure, however, the unbalancing effect is difficult to resolve, even for the specialist. Treasure is, by definition, unusual, special, and a tantalising aspect of it is often its lack of background. For example, the great Anglo-Saxon royal treasure, found at Sutton Hoo in Suffolk over fifty years ago, necessarily revolutionised views of kingship and society in seventh century East Anglia; but the succeeding fifty years have done relatively little to fill in the background of how that treasure came to be amassed, and views of Anglo-Saxon East Anglia would not be greatly different from those of fifty years ago, were it not that the Sutton Hoo find has to be taken into account.

So it has been with the Cuerdale Hoard. When a hoard of Viking silver, heavier than any other, with the exception of certain Russian finds, is found, the discovery must have its effect on the view of the period (tenth century) and area (North-West England) concerned. Indeed, the peculiar status of the treasure is emphasised by its coverage here in a separate chapter. Locating the background of that treasure has been somewhat more difficult than describing it.

Let us look, first, at the finding itself.[1] The discovery was made late in the afternoon of Friday, 15th May, 1840. Workmen were working on the bank of the River Ribble in the small township of Cuerdale, south of Preston. They were on the land of Cuerdale Hall and not very far from it. Cuerdale Hall belonged at that time to William, the then current head of the Assheton family, which had owned it since 1614. The family home of this branch of the Asshetons had been, since 1558, at Downham Hall, not very far from Clitheroe and sixteen miles further up the Ribble valley from Cuerdale. This is still the case today, when the family is headed by the second Lord Clitheroe, his father having been ennobled in 1955.

The workmen concerned were repairing the bank of the River Ribble. It is not quite clear whether they were repairing an *earlier* defence against erosion or creating a new one. Hawkins, the numismatist who first published the find, clearly says that they were getting earth to fill in behind an earlier stone defence which had been overwhelmed and eroded from the back by the river. A slight element of doubt is provided by the plan, produced by the Duchy of Lancaster for the Treasure Trove inquest, which refers to '*New* Stone Wall' at the extreme edge of the river. It is certain, however, that the workmen were digging for suitable filling material some forty yards back from the edge of the river.

Whether or not it was new in 1840, what is presumably the stone defence in question can be seen at Cuerdale today (figure 28). A stone wall leads down to the river bank at the upstream end of the bend near the Hall, and continues, diminishing in number of courses as it enters the water, to form a straight line like a bow string to the river's curve corresponding to the bow. Today, as

Figure 28. The river defences, now eroded, which were under construction at the time of the discovery of the Cuerdale Hoard in 1840.

probably in 1840, the river has won a round in the battle, and the stones are several feet out into the water.

There does not seem to be much doubt as to what happened. One of the workmen noticed something in the soil being loaded by another into a barrow. When the peculiar objects, apparently at first thought to be shells, were recognised as coins, there was, needless to say, great excitement. Whether the noise was really loud enough to carry to the Hall, as has been said, or whether the news of the discovery was actually conveyed thither, it came to the notice of Mr Assheton's steward or hind, Jonathan Richardson.

He was clearly a man of some character. He had been involved in the discovery, two years earlier, of a Bronze Age axe head in the same field, and now his authority and personal magnetism were sufficient for him to disabuse the workmen of the idea that because they had indeed found treasure, 'finders keepers' applied.

Richardson's first duty was to his employers, William Assheton, who was then in Rome. He thought, quite rightly, that the landowner was likely to have a legal claim to the find, and acted on his behalf by collecting the whole find and taking it to Cuerdale Hall. We are told that he allowed each of the workmen to keep a single 'souvenir' coin, and also that others were taken away from the site by stealth, the favourite story being of twenty or more in a workman's boots.

The find was washed and scrubbed with a birch broom at the Hall, and a special box was made for it, and the following morning it was all taken to the Old Bank in Preston, that is the bank of Messrs. Pedder, Fleetwood and Pedder, which was on the site at present occupied by the Trustee Savings Bank, opposite the parish church.

Descriptions of the discovery make it clear that the find was enclosed in some way in lead. Indeed, at least one fragment of the lead has been preserved (figure 29). What is

Figure 29. Piece of the lead (?lining of the) chest in which the Cuerdale Hoard was contained.

not certain is whether the lead was the sole container or whether it formed the lining of some kind of wooden chest, which seems more probable. It has even been suggested that it *enclosed* the box. While finds from, for example, Whithorn, make it clear that the technology was available to make a large sheet-lead container at that time, it seems more likely that the container was a lead-lined chest and that traces of the wood, if seen at all, were not understood or were disregarded. From the point of view of the inquest, where the presence of a container was material evidence in deciding whether or not the find was Treasure Trove, the lead was quite sufficient to show that there had been one.

If William Assheton had a claim to the find as the landowner, the other claimant was the Crown, represented in this case by the Duchy of Lancaster. The law of Treasure Trove[2] stems from medieval kings' chronic shortage of cash, and its provisions, enshrined in Statute Law from Common Law, were not designed for the preservation of archaeological material or information. Generally, when treasure found is declared to be Treasure Trove, it is forfeit to the Crown, but in certain cases the 'Franchise of Treasure Trove' has been bestowed elsewhere by the Crown, and this is the case within the Duchy of Lancaster. Treasure Trove found in Lancashire is still forfeit to the Queen 'in right of her Duchy'.

It fell, therefore, to the law officers of the Duchy to prepare their side of the case as against that of William Assheton. It is, of course, strictly speaking, inaccurate to paint this situation as an adversarial one, for the proceedings were to be, as they still would be today, before a coroner and a jury, the latter charged to hear the evidence and decide the answers to a number of questions.

The inquest was held, some three months after the find was made, in the Bull Inn, Preston, later to become the Bull and Royal. The delay was caused, not as it might well have been today by the necessity to study the find closely, but by the illness of William Assheton's wife, which necessitated a longer stay in Rome than had been planned. The Coroner, Mr Hargreaves, empanelled a jury of sixteen, all men, of course. They included two described as Gentlemen and thirteen tradesmen, of whom two were upholsterers, and the remainder a watchmaker; a cotton spinner; a printer; a gardener; a draper; a stationer; a hosier; a gilder; a tobacconist; a hatter; and a pawnbroker. The station in life of the foreman of the jury is not mentioned, but he alone in the list of jurors rates the title of 'Mr'. The Duchy was represented by its Attorney General, Thomas Flower Ellis, advised by its Solicitor General, John Teasdale. Mr Assheton was represented by John Addison. A rather fine document recording the jury's verdict is preserved in the Duchy archives, and it is amusing that its description of the nature of the find (one of the questions on which the jury had to decide) is highly schematic and highly inaccurate. For a variety of reasons which will become apparent, the precise contents of the hoard will never be known, but certainly nothing was present in the neat round numbers of the Verdict's 'one thousand Bars one thousand Ingots one thousand pieces of Silver ...' and the 'one thousand Chains' were not present at all!

The jury decided that its first duty was to view the site of the find, and this they did. The site, said the *Preston Chronicle* in reporting the find on 23rd May, 1840, had been 'more zealously scratched than any dunghill in the best populated poultry yard', so its reporter was clearly justified in saying 'The circumstance has created a lively sensation in the neighbourhood'.

When the jury came to consider the evidence, they had, according to the *Preston Chronicle*, to contend with 'a great deal of very dry matter' with which the newspaper, regrettably, decided not to burden its readers. Considering the length at which much seemingly 'dry matter' was reported in the mid nineteenth century, this omission is almost suspicious. One wonders whether the reporter spent some of the period of the inquest in another part of the Bull Inn, or, if that is felt to be defamatory to his shade, if the poor man had to cope with other, more routine, reporting at the same time.

The jury heard the Attorney General of the Duchy contend that the hoard met the criteria for Treasure Trove – 'Money or coin, plate or bullion, hidden in the ground or other secret place, of which the owner is unknown'. Mr Addison, for Mr Assheton, contended that the treasure had either been abandoned (as opposed to hidden) or had been washed ashore (more than two thirds of a hundredweight of it, apart from the lead and a wooden casket, if such there were!) at a time when the Ribble was navigable as far upstream as Ribchester. This latter idea had been started by John Whitaker, the historian of Manchester, in the late eighteenth century in order to explain the presence of Anchor Hill at Ribchester – a name which is almost certainly derived from the former siting there of an anchorite's cell.

The ultimate verdict of the jury was that the find was indeed Treasure Trove and thus forfeit to Queen Victoria, still less than four years on the throne, as incumbent of the Duchy of Lancaster. The verdict, exactly what it would have been today, had very different consequences then as compared to the present. Today the advising authority would have been the British Museum, which would also

have been the receiving institution, and the finders would have been handsomely rewarded, by an *ex gratia* payment rather than by right. The landowner would have received nothing. In 1840 custom was different. The finders, who are not even named in the newspaper reports (Thomas Marsden is named as their representative in the Verdict) disappear totally from view, though their names are given in one publication: they were, apart from Marsden: Henry Bennett; Edward Brown; William Dawson; James Holding; Thomas Horrocks; Thomas Parkinson; Thomas Southworth; William Teasdale; William Valentine; John Walmsley; James Walne; John Walton and Ambrose Woods. Even Richardson, but for whose praiseworthy efforts the find would have been instantly dispersed, received only twenty pounds. Assheton, when the Duchy came to distribute the hoard, received a selection of coins and silver in a rosewood case, together with a gold Coronation Medal. To his great credit, Assheton made sure that Richardson received, from these, a small selection of items in a velvet-lined box.

Having seized the treasure and allowed Edward Hawkins of the British Museum to examine it and select for the British Museum, the Duchy Office, in the person of one Dawes Danvers, its Clerk of the Council, set about dispersing it to collectors. Despite pious hopes, allegedly based on remarks made by the Attorney General of the Duchy and reported in the *Preston Chronicle*, little of it came to local institutions. The Preston Institution for the Diffusion of Knowledge acquired some coins, but its successor, the Harris Museum and Art Gallery, still does not have any other silver from the hoard. Samples, varying in size, went to a number of museums, apart from the British Museum, including the Ashmolean Museum, Oxford and the Hunterian Coin Cabinet, Glasgow. In addition, for several years thereafter, many individuals, some from abroad, wrote to the Duchy requesting Cuerdale material and received donations. These totalled over 170 individuals and institutions. Although some record was kept, it was of a very rudimentary nature – 'Two coins, one armring' – which accounts for the ultimate imprecision in the record of the contents of the hoard.

It is also almost certain that other Cuerdale material was acquired locally – whether by discoveries made in the 'dunghill scratchings' mentioned earlier or because Richardson's efforts were less thorough than had been thought. In fact, some of the 'escapes' derived from a selection of coins which Richardson extracted from the hoard on behalf of Assheton. The rarities which this selection contained make it clear that Richardson acted with expert advice. Although his action was, strictly speaking, illegal, it was acknowledged later that Richardson's motives were altruistic. This could not be said of several other removals from the hoard, almost all of coins, which can be demonstrated with varying degrees of precision when the coins turn up elsewhere. However, because many of the coins in the hoard were otherwise unknown, or almost so, many saleroom lots in the last 150 years have been identified as 'Cuerdale strays', though this identification, of course, contains the possibility of a circular argument.

What, then, was actually found? The record of the hoard includes three main elements: Coins; Ingots; other objects of silver, many of these in fragments. In addition, four bone pins and a bone needle are attributed to the hoard. These are the only non-silver items.

Coins

The coins are, of course, vitally important in any consideration of the hoard because they can be used to date its deposition with reasonable precision. Further, we have a better idea of the numismatic contents of the hoard than of the rest because Hawkins was a numismatist. Even he made no complete list, and,

of course, no one at the time knew much about the dating or other aspects of the rest of the items in the hoard. Minor uncertainties about coin issues made over a millennium ago have produced slightly varying dates for the deposition, that accepted for some considerable time being 903, which was attractively close to the date of the expulsion of the Norse from Dublin. Expert opinion has, however, now swung back to a date widely held somewhat earlier – c. 905. This and other considerations, such as the origin of the metalwork in the hoard, to which we will return, seem to rule out the possibility that the hoard came with its owner or owners from Ireland in 902. There is, on the other hand, a real possibility that the hoard represents wealth gathered with a view to reversing the expulsion. It may well be that the fact that there are two main elements within the hoard, one from the west (specifically Ireland) and the other from the east, means that we have a hoard brought out of Dublin, or at least Ireland, reinforced with silver gathered in the York area.

At any rate, many of the coins came westwards to Cuerdale. Nowhere to the north and west of Cuerdale had a coin-*using* economy in the tenth century. The coins (figure 30) can be divided into a number of groups, and conclusions can be drawn, or at least ideas put forward, about a number of aspects of the hoard as a result of their study. The prime mover in recent years in this study was the late Christopher Blunt, and it is his work which laid the framework for our modern view of the numismatic element of the hoard. Since his death, his mantle in this respect has fallen on Miss Marion Archibald of the British Museum, and it is largely their joint view of the coinage which is here reported. It is necessary to make this clear because the study of numismatics is so specialised that the non-specialist such as the present writer can only summarise what the specialists decide. Nonetheless, responsibility for the summary remains with the author, and neither

Figure 30. Two representative coins from the Cuerdale Hoard, A CNVT REX and a CVNNETTI. (By courtesy of the Harris Museum, Preston)

Christopher Blunt nor Marion Archibald is responsible for any peculiarities or personal views which may creep in.

There were, then, five main groups of coins represented in the hoard, and Blunt's researches led him to the conclusion that the total number of coins probably lay between 7,000 and 7,500. The official (and highly inaccurate) account of the inquest gave the total as 8,000, while Hawkins, in what remains the only 'complete' publication of the hoard, gave 'six or seven thousand'. Other writers have suggested that the total was as high as 10,000, but this cannot be supported by the evidence.

Of each group of coins we can ask a number of questions, of which the most useful are: – What is their origin? What is their date of issue, particularly that of the latest coin as a clue to the date of deposition of the hoard? And what was their probable route to Cuerdale?

Numerically the largest group by some way, with nearly 5,000 coins, were the Insular (i.e. British) Viking coins, and of these the majority were apparently struck at York. They bear legends (i.e. inscriptions) frequently including variants of the name of York, deriving from its Roman name of Eboracum, in forms such as EBRAICE CIVI, often blundered (i.e. rendered inaccurately, presumably by a monyer who was illiterate or barely literate). Other inscriptions frequent among these coins are SIEFRED, CNVT REX and CVNNETTI together with brief phrases taken from the Liturgy, such as DOMINVS D(EV)S REX and MIRABILIA FECIT. Much smaller numbers occur of ALVALDVS and ORNSAFORDA.

Attempts have been made in the past to identify some of the legends as mint names. It should, perhaps, be explained that many coins of this period carry one or more of the following pieces of information in the inscription: the name of the person for whom they were issued; the moneyer responsible; and the mint at which the coin was struck. Coins seldom carry more than one representational symbol – a bird, a sword or the like – and seldom a head. All, incidentally, are silver pennies, this denomination, at a weight of 22½ grains (240 to the Troy pound of 5,400 grains) having been introduced at the end of the eighth century. Very occasionally there are halfpennies. Generally, if a halfpenny was required it was obtained literally by halving a penny. No other course was open from the Norman Conquest to the mid-thirteenth century.

To return to the question of mint names, EBRAICE has generally been taken as York, though Evreux has also been suggested. ORSNAFORDA has been identified as Oxford, though without certainty. Even less certainly, CVNNETTI has been attributed to Condé, but really remains an enigma. ORSNAFORDA has also been put forward as an alternative name for York, but again this is improbable.

On the subject of mints, it is seldom that a mint can be demonstrated to have existed at this period otherwise than by the existence of coins struck at it. Thus the objection that no mint was known at York in the early tenth century was really a poor objection to the attribution of the EBRAICE coins to that city. Nevertheless, the discovery in York in recent years of some of the impedimenta of coin-making has generated some thoughts about tenth century coin issue. The material consists of two coin dies and two lead trial-pieces, and dates from nearly half a century after the deposition date of the Cuerdale Hoard. What makes it particularly interesting and thought-provoking, however, is that one of the dies was apparently that of a Chester moneyer, and the premises in which they were found did not seem likely itself to have been a mint. It may indicate that specialist die-making might take place away from mint sites.

If the mint names on these coins are sometimes obscure, even the personages named are not always known historically. CNVT REX, for example, is not the well-known King Canute of legend. He reigned in the eleventh century. A possible candidate at the end of the ninth century is Guthred of York, who may have adopted Cnut as a baptismal name in the same way that Guthrum became Athelstan in the mid-tenth century.

There are two series of Viking coins issued at the beginning of the tenth century, one bearing the name of St Edmund and the other

of St Peter. The first is well represented at Cuerdale, by something nearing 2,000 coins, the second not at all. Precise knowledge of the dates of issue of these coins would help in dating the Cuerdale Hoard, but that knowledge we do not have. In fact, here we meet one of the problems of the hoard. Many of its coins are unique to the hoard or were previously represented only in one or two finds. As a result, the hoard itself is taken as important evidence to date an issue, and a circular argument results. As examples of the way in which the Cuerdale find altered perceptions, previously only one English site (Harkirke, see p. 42–45) had yielded one CVNNETTI coin, the only recorded ORSNAFORDA had been found in the Ouse at York in 1740 and only a dozen or so St Edmund coins were known, all different from any in the Cuerdale Hoard.

These St Edmund coins have been regarded as, and called, a memorial issue, but on any acceptable dating of the Cuerdale Hoard, must have been issued within thirty years of the royal saint's death. This seems a surprisingly rapid growth of a cult, and, while the coins are to some extent paralleled by the St Peter coins of York and some in the name of St Martin from Lincoln, neither of these two saints was so recently dead. It is said that the St Edmund coins were minted in East Anglia, by moneyers with largely Frankish names, but no convincing mint site has yet been suggested. Some of the coins of Siefred were minted at Quentovic in Francia, so it is even possible that the St Edmund coins were too.

This brings us to the second of our five groups – the Carolingian coins. These, like the Viking coins, have two main sub-groups, those minted in western France and those minted further east and south. Not surprisingly, there were more of the former (c. 900 as against c. 100 from what are now eastern France, Switzerland, Germany, Austria and Italy, together with the Netherlands). While the mint names and rulers' names are often readily readable, their use for dating purposes is restricted by the frequent repetition of royal names and our limited knowledge of their sequence.

The Carolingian Empire, named from its ruler at the beginning of the ninth century, Charles the Great (Charlemagne, or Carolus in Latin) was of wide extent at the end of the ninth and the beginning of the tenth centuries. It covered most of what is today France, Germany, the Netherlands, Austria, Switzerland and Italy. Coins were issued, of course, in the names of various princes, kings and even Popes, in addition to that of the titular Emperor. Sometimes difficulties occur with these coins because names of rulers were repeated, sometimes because a particular type of coin continued to be issued after the death of the person in whose name it was issued.

The coins from the so-called Middle Kingdom, which was the successor of the territory allotted to Lothar, Charlemagne's grandson, at the Treaty of Verdun in 843, number about 100 and include some which must have been struck between 901 and 903. Others, related, which date from after 902, and might have been expected to be present, are missing. Those coins from western France, though more numerous at about 900, are not so useful for dating purposes. Most of these Carolingian coins, incidentally, were presumably the fruits of late ninth century Viking raiding up the rivers of western Europe.

Third among the coin groups to be considered, and the only remaining large group, are the Anglo-Saxon coins. These are predominantly issues of King Alfred, whose reign ceased in 899. Of his successor, Edward the Elder, there are fewer than 50 coins. These include some which must have been struck a little after the beginning of the reign, but none of another type which cannot be earlier than 910. This gap, between 899+ and 910, must cover the deposition date of the hoard, but these coins do not help to narrow it. It may well be that the Anglo-Saxon element among the coins got into the hoard in some slightly

odd way, for although there are well over a thousand Anglo-Saxon coins, there is virtually no other Anglo-Saxon metalwork.

The remaining coins idenified in the hoard are from more exotic locations. First, there are four Scandinavian coins from Hedeby (then Danish, though now in Germany) and one from Byzantium. They provide virtually no assistance in the matter of dating, but are interesting when the question of the sources of the hoard is considered. The other group of coins really are exotic. These are about fifty Arabic dihrems. These coins, of which many similar have been found in Scandinavia, resulted from trade, much of it up the rivers which run into the Baltic and down those running into the Black Sea. The reverse part of this trade would presumably have been in untraceable organic material such as furs or amber and also slaves. It might be assumed that many of the Arabic coins were converted by the Vikings into silver objects such as brooches or armrings, or into ingots. Trace element analysis, however does not greatly support this idea, though mixing of melts soon destroys the potential of such analysis.

These dihrems, like western coins of the same period, carry such information as the name of the person for whom they were issued and the mint at which they were struck. The latter show an astonishingly wide distribution, reflecting, no doubt both the widespread nature of the Arabic world in which they originally circulated and the breadth of contacts of the Viking traders to whom they passed. Eight different mints are represented, ranging from one near Cordova in Spain to another not far from Kabul in what is now Afghanistan. One piece of information which these coins do carry, however, which is not reflected on contemporary western coinage, is the date of issue. This, expressed of course in terms of the Muslim calendar, is readily converted to years AD, but it is singularly frustrating that the precise date of what must be the latest coin among them is not legible on the coin. The others, in terms of what is present and (like some other coin groups) what might be expected to be present but is actually missing, again give a tantalising gap just after AD 900.

Ingots

Turning, next, from the coins to the ingots, we encounter another form in which the Vikings used silver in the mechanics of trade (figure 31). The vast majority of such ingots were cast in simple one-piece moulds consisting of hollows cut in stone. We have already encountered some ingots in considering coin-hoards in the last chapter. There, the comparison in shape and size was made between most Viking silver ingots and cigars, the simile being apt in that there is some

variation in the size of both, but the overall range (cigarillo to Corona) is not dissimilar. In addition to these ingots, the Cuerdale Hoard contained a number of rather larger ingots of different shape cast in a mould which had a cross cut into it. To these, otherwise unknown, we shall return. The ingots as a whole form a considerable proportion of the silver – numerically about one third and slightly less by weight.

The effective use of ingots in the mechanism of trade, however, requires two or three other factors to be in place. Firstly, there is the matter of the weight of the silver. This could be dealt with in one or both of two ways. Either the ingots would have to conform to a system of weights or their use would have to be accompanied by the use of scales. We know that the latter existed in Viking

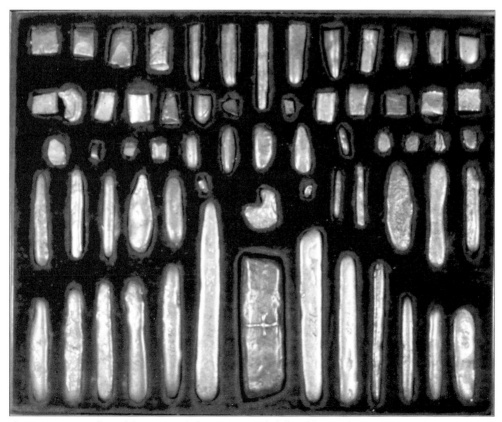

Figure 31. A group of Cuerdale ingots, including a cross-marked ('Mark') ingot, bottom centre.

society, some of them of ingenious folding types, but presumably these would be used primarily to balance weights against loose items of hacksilver (see below, p. 63). An attempt was made at the time of the discovery of the Cuerdale Hoard to suggest that the large cross-marked ingots were equivalent to a specific weight of silver – a 'mark' – and they thus acquired the name of Mark Ingots. More recent work has identified the average weight of the Mark Ingots as ⅔ of that of an Anglo-Saxon, or possibly Anglo-Scandinavian, 'account' pound.

Other ingots were clearly frequently subdivided, there being many, both in the Cuerdale Hoard and from elsewhere, which have been cut, presumably with a hammer and chisel.

The other requirement of any system of barter using bullion as an exchange mechanism is that the silver should be of a certain fineness. This, of course, is the basis of the use of coins, where the design of the coin itself, together with the name of the authority (king, etc.) issuing the coin, form, or should form, a guarantee of weight and fineness. In other words, coins are small, self-certifying ingots.

Lacking such guarantees, the users of Viking ingots had to obtain their proof of fineness otherwise, and it is one of the achievements of Professor James Graham Campbell to draw our attention to how this was done. The answer was by the use of nicking. Both ingots and fragmented silver ornaments (hacksilver) frequently display nicks where a sharp knife-like blade has been driven into the silver by a hammer blow. The skill which must have been possessed by the Viking trader, but which we lack, was the ability to assess the fineness of the silver by the readiness or otherwise with which the blade penetrated the metal. Of course, the detection of a total forgery, such as one made of lead, would not be difficult, but the existence of the ingots themselves shows that facilities existed widely for melting metal, and

the adulteration of silver by the addition of a small proportion of base metal would not presumably have been too difficult. The same considerations show that the traders must have been able to detect such adulteration, otherwise we would not find the large number of nicks which we do on some pieces of silver. That is to say, the process was widely used and therefore it must have worked.

Coins, incidentally, were regularly tested in the same way, though by the use of a sharp point rather than a blade. The process is therefore referred to as 'pecking' in the case of coins as against 'nicking' ingots and ornaments. The number of nicks or pecks on any given piece of silver, or better on a group of items, is some index of how much circulation they had had. Conversely, objects without such mutilation are more likely to have been freshly manufactured when incorporated into the hoard.

The large cross-marked ingots are of some interest. Some scepticism has already been expressed as to their relationship to a system of weights, but their distinctive nature proves two other points in relation to the hoard. First, it is obvious that ingot-moulds were re-used; the existence of the cross-marked ingots all cast in the same mould alone shows this. In addition, some of these ingots show a diagonal mark which betrays the fact that the mould for them had cracked during the sequence of castings necessary to produce a series of identical ingots.

The other point relates to our incomplete knowledge of the contents of the hoard. These distinctive ingots are the sole artifacts of which we know the precise number occurring in the hoard. There were sixteen, but, of these, we can today locate only twelve.

It is almost needless to say that the precise origin of ingots cannot be determined. Ingot moulds have been discovered in, for example, Ireland, but the technology both of the manufacture of the moulds and that of the casting of the ingots in them, is so simple that it could have taken place anywhere.

Other Silver

Inability to determine an origin, of vary degrees of precision, is, however, not so much a problem for the third class of object represented in the hoard. This consistcd of a very wide range of silver ornaments, almost all of which had been treated in such a way as to make it clear that they had been regarded solely as so much weight of silver. In a majority of cases, this means that they had been cut up, though some had merely been crushed or folded so as to take up less space.

At this point we may make a digression to consider a name for such ornaments-to-be-used-as-bullion. The German word *hacksilber* has been adopted for this, though it has its detractors. These include those who have an aversion to using a foreign word at all and those who point out that the 'hack-' element of the word, being related to, but not identical in meaning to, the English verb of the same spelling, suggests that a much more violent process was employed in fragmenting the ornaments than was probably the case.

A means of meeting the first of these objections, though not the second, has been found in the coinage of the English neologism *hacksilver*, thereby producing a technical term not normally requiring the use of italics, inverted commas or other typographical selectivity. It seems to the writer that if there exists a linguistic gap which can otherwise only be filled by circumlocution considerations of language purity and inexact equivalence of what sounds to be the meaning are not sufficient reasons to veto the creation of a word which fills that gap. As in the case of names for types of brooches, those to whom the use of the word is a convenience will quickly learn its meaning, while the possible occasional misleading of those less closely concerned with the subject is of comparatively little account. Cut up, or otherwise mutilated silver ornaments, then, are hacksilver for the purposes of this account.

As has already been suggested, the usefulness of the hacksilver in the hoard is that, in many cases, the origin of the ornaments can either be determined, or, at least, named wth some degree of probability and their route to Cuerdale suggested. This fact immediately brings to light the interesting situation that the origins of the coinage and of the hacksilver in the Cuerdale Hoard are almost completely mutually exclusive. Not only are there, obviously, no coins originating in the non-coin-using areas to the north and west of Cuerdale, but that is where the hacksilver does originate and little of it originates where the coins do. The very rare exceptions to the last portion of the previous sentence have the interesting additional qualification that they must have been quite old at the time of the deposition of the hoard, and therefore probably followed a different route to Cuerdale from that of the coins.

To give one or two examples, we may return, for a moment, to the coins. We have seen that the mints at which the Kufic (Arabic) coins were struck were far-flung (p. 60), but the routes by which these coins reached Cuerdale have been convincingly shown to have been *via* Norway, Scotland and then the Irish Sea. In the latter stages of their journeys they were probably accompanied by a number of the fragments of so-called 'Permian' rings and of arm-rings and penannular brooches of Baltic origin which are present.

For the other Scandinavian material in the hoard it is not possible to identify a route with certainty, but there are a few hints. For example, there are a number of objects of distinctively Danish origin – coins from Hedeby, ribbon bracelets and certain types of arm ring – and Norwegian – trefoil-headed pins – where Cuerdale is the sole British find-spot or where such objects can be shown to have reached north east England (their only other British localities) not before ten to twenty years after the date of the Cuerdale deposition, while parallels at the right date are known from Ireland. As in the case of the other items just discussed, the suggestion persists of a longer route to Cuerdale than the direct one. This conclusion of a north westerly origin for much of the hacksilver is supported by the fact that as much as 25 per cent of the bullion consists of Hiberno-Viking arm rings.

In addition to the items just considered, the hoard included what might be called a few strays. A couple of pieces of Pictish metalwork fall into this category as do the few pieces of Anglo-Saxon metalwork. These latter contrast sharply with the thousand or more Anglo-Saxon coins, which fact, when taken with the lack of pecking on the latter, suggests that the coins were freshly minted at the time of deposition while the metalwork scraps had probably long been in circulation as loot.

The Amassing of the Hoard

We have now considered the circumstances surrounding the discovery of the hoard and some of the contents of the hoard and their implications. This leads us to the more general question of what is implied by the existence of the hoard. First, it must be made clear that it was almost the heaviest hoard of Viking silver ever discovered anywhere, and that includes hoards found in Scandinavia. Only in Russia has anything surpassed it. To give some idea of the degree by which it surpassed others, the next nearest in weight from Britain after Cuerdale's c. 40kg. (nearly two thirds of a hundredweight, for those more used to older measures) was the hoard from Skaill (Orkney) which weighed c. 8 kg., that is one fifth of the weight of Cuerdale. While there is a hoard from Carrick (Lough Ennell) which weighed c. 32kg, that hoard consisted of non-Scandinavian ingots, though its date is not greatly different from that of Cuerdale. Next down the scale from the British Isles is the hoard known as Dysart Is. No.4, at under a kilogram. Scandinavian

hoards range up to c. 8.75kg. in Skasne and c. 8kg. on Gotland.

All of that establishes the superiority in weight of Cuerdale to that of any other hoard found, which is sufficient to indicate for it an exceptional status. It was not, of course, necessarily the heaviest hoard in its own time. Collections of silver of this magnitude *may* have travelled regularly in the ninth and tenth centuries. It is possible that Cuerdale's uniqueness lies in its not having been recovered by its rightful owners in the tenth century. Whatever the causes of its assembly and deposition – matters to which we will return shortly – it is indeed somewhat difficult to imagine the circumstances which led to its being lost. The weight alone must have ensured that its existence was known to a number of people. That its guardians as it travelled and was concealed (under what threat or other circumstances?) were all somehow eliminated and that no one else knew enough of the situation to recover the treasure is strange, but must nonetheless have been the case. Were it not so, William Assheton's workmen would not have had their great surprise in May, 1840.

Why, then, and where, was the collection assembled and what was happening or about to happen to it? These are obviously inter-related questions, and the key to their answer must lie in the date of deposition. Given that the size of the hoard implies that it had some kind of corporate or quasi-official ownership, and that there were two great centres of Viking political power in the British Isles at the very beginning of the tenth century, the hoard's existence must surely be linked to the history of York and Dublin.

The most significant event in the first years of the tenth century to affect either was the expulsion of the Norsemen from Dublin in 902. The character of the hoard and the sources of its various components, which we have considered, would all fit with the suggestion that its assembly was in some way connected with an attempt to reverse the expulsion. It cannot have been either a treasure chest removed from Dublin or the "war-chest of the Viking army", a favourite explanation in the nineteenth century, though some of the non-coin material may have come to England with the expelled Norse.

It is surely certain that the hoard was concealed during a pause on a journey. But a journey in which direction and where from and to? North-south or the reverse is, of course, not impossible, but east-west or west-east seems much more probable. If it came to crossing the Pennines in the tenth century, the Roman roads would surely have largely constituted the route (figure 32). Only three such cross-Pennine roads existed – that through the Tyne gap; that across Stainmore; and that connecting the legionary fortresses of York and Chester. This latter road crossed the hills between Tadcaster and Ribchester. The traveller actually making a York to Chester journey in Roman times would then have turned south, *via* Manchester. Our putative Vikings would not have wanted to go to Chester if Dublin had been their ultimate objective. The Ribble estuary, however, could, as James Graham Campbell and Nick Higham have established, have provided a suitable naval base or roadstead in which to assemble a re-invasion fleet. Might we even

suggest that whatever disaster led to the loss of the Cuerdale hoard, or that loss itself, was a contributory factor in the fifteen year gap which actually ensued between the expulsion and the re-establishment, apparently on a new site, of Viking Dublin?

Two further points are worthy of comment. We have seen how, if some part, specifically the coin element, of the hoard had travelled from the general vicinity of York, it may well have travelled on Roman roads as far as Ribchester. Further travel down the Ribble valley towards the area of Cuerdale would not have been too difficult. The Roman road westwards from Ribchester towards Kirkham might have been used, though that would have brought the hoard to the vicinity of Fulwood, north of Preston, where that road interesected the south-north road from the site at Walton-le-Dale towards Lancaster. In that case, it is difficult to see why the hoard was concealed on the south side of the river at Cuerdale. That spot is, however, not only one at which the river is fordable, but, perhaps more relevantly, is near what is likely to have been the head of the tide. In other words, it was a possible trans-shipment point. Such considerations are difficult to be sure about because so much alteration has taken place to the flow of the river both above and below Cuerdale.

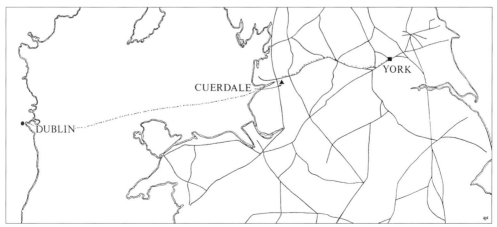

Figure 32. Part of Northern England and the Irish Sea, showing Roman roads, York, Cuerdale and Dublin.

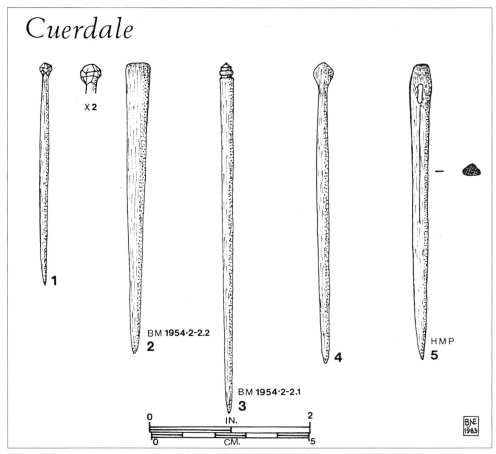

Figure 33. Four bone pins and a bone needle from the Cuerdale Hoard. Nos 1, 3 and 4 are Roman.

A hint that the Roman road in the vicinity of Clitheroe was in use at least until well after maintenance of it had ceased came when a small section of it was examined prior to the construction of the Whalley-Clitheroe by-pass. The line of the road was then found to be represented by a considerable hollow in the limestone, the orginal road surface presumably having been at some distance above it.

Another point which the writer has adduced in favour of movement by at least part of the hoard from east to west concerns a group of four bone pins and a bone needle (figure 33) which, though not recorded at the time of the discovery, were kept in a local family, with the remains of a nineteenth century label attributing them to Cuerdale, until 1941. They were then examined and published by no less an authority than Sir Thomas Kendrick. This publication gave them the status of Viking pins, but there seems to be no doubt that three of the pins are Roman in origin (Edwards 1984). The fourth is both much simpler than the others and is paler in colour, suggesting that it may have been made later. If, then, three of the pins are Roman (the needle is not datable), they might well have originated in York, where plenty such are found. Nowhere west of Cuerdale is likely to have provided them. Their function, of course, is unknown, but one suggestion made is that they may have been used to fasten money-bags, though no such practice is actually recorded.

The date of the Viking expulsion from Dublin is, of course, close to, and maybe even directly related to, the often accepted date of the commencement of Norse settlement in north-west England. In considering this it is necessary to be careful, for the date of that event is by no means firmly established. A reference, far from totally reliable, has been quoted to date the settlement of Ingimund and his followers in Wirral, and that, in turn, has been taken to mean that Norse settlement in Lancashire and Cumbria began at about the same date. While there is little evidence to gainsay that conclusion, there is not a great deal to support it either. The pagan-style burials described in Chapter 2 might be thought to pre-date the Christianisation of the Norse, but some doubts have been thrown on this deduction in Chapter 2, and in any case the Christianisation itself is neither independently dated nor even, possibly, susceptible of very precise dating.

As far as the Cuerdale Hoard is concerned, we can at least say this: if the suggestion that its existence is related to the possible use of the Ribble estuary as a base for the Norse recovery of Dublin, it would scarcely have been hidden at Cuerdale had the inhabitants of the nearby coastline been in any way hostile.

Envoi

Today, the site of the discovery is marked by a small stone pillar bearing the simple inscription 'SITE OF/CUERDALE/HOARD/15 MAY 1840'. That stone was unveiled by Sir Ralph Assheton, the father of the present Lord Clitheroe, on 5th October, 1948, the Second World War having precluded any marking of the centenary of the find. The stone is the latest of a series of markers for the site. By the time of the inquest, a stake had been placed there, and this was later replaced by a willow tree. This was of considerable size when it was illustrated by local artist Edward Beattie in the *Preston Guardian* in 1906 (figure 34). Its fate was recorded in a photograph preserved in a

Figure 34. Edward Beattie's 1895 drawing of the willow tree marking the site of the Cuerdale find, published in the Preston Guardian in 1906.

Cuerdale scrapbook compiled by a Preston antiquary, James Charnley. This shows a broken stump, with a telling caption 'Cuerdale Willow Felled by a Storm'.

Notes

1. No 'complete' publication of the Cuerdale Hoard exists, nor is one now possible, though Edward Hawkins did produce two general papers (Hawkins 1843, 1847). The nearest possible approach is forthcoming in the British Museum's catalogue of Viking silver under the editorship of James Graham Campbell. In the meantime, reference should be made to Graham Campbell (ed.) 1992 and Philpott (ed. Graham Campbell) 1992.

2. Statements about Treasure Trove in this chapter relate to the state of affairs prior to the implementation of the Treasure Act, 1996.

CHAPTER SIX

Sculpture

On a distribution map of Viking age artifacts from North West England (see figure 9), the largest number of symbols relates to sculpture. That this should be the case is not altogether surprising. Stone has durable qualities not possessed by, for example, metal; and many stone sculptures, whether broken up or kept in their entirety, thus lend themselves to re-use more readily than do artifacts made of other materials. Many of the surviving Viking sculptures have demonstrable Christian connections; however, such connections do not on their own account for their survival; for many survived re-used simply as building material rather than on account of any symbolism or significance. Today we have no justification for any feelings of surprise or disapproval at such treatment of Christian art; for in our own age it is by no means uncommon for Christian gravestones to be cleared from our churchyards and re-used, either broken up to form a rubble base or kept entire and used to create a pathway.

Whatever vicissitudes have befallen our pre-Conquest stone sculpture and resulted in the survival of what must be only a small proportion of what was there originally, for our present purpose we must define what we are talking about and what we are not. In some sense 'Viking sculpture' is almost a contradiction in terms, for the carving of stone crosses was not a Viking activity originally. The runestones of Sweden and such items as the 'Harald Bluetooth' stone at Jelling show us Scandinavians decorating and inscribing stone, but the result was mostly quite unlike anything we have in Britain, and, more particularly, in north west England. Here in England the idea of the free-standing stone cross seems to have sprung from the mind of an Anglo-Saxon, and, whatever the source of the idea of the stone cross itself, we can identify probable ultimate sources for elements in their decoration such as vine scroll, interlace, spirals, and 'Greek Key'. We can also suggest plausible means by which the knowledge of such artistic motifs might have reached the Anglo-Saxons in the eighth and ninth centuries.

When Scandinavian influence began to affect everyday life in these islands (as opposed to influencing military activity) artistic ideas from the north began to alter various aspects of craftsmanship too. We can thus see the 'arrival' of Norsemen reflected in the imposition of elements of their taste on pre-existing insular taste. How, then, do we identify the Scandinavian taste, particularly when it first begins and represents only a small part in the design?

The answer to that question must be 'with difficulty' because, as in the case of so much else, there was much common ground between the Germanic inhabitants whom the Norse found in Britain and the Norsemen themselves. If they, the Norse, were not great carvers of stone, they were certainly artists and carvers of wood. Wherever wood is preserved in Scandinavian contexts – in the Oseberg ship burial and the wooden churches of Norway, and at sites like Dublin and York – we find relief carving in enthusiastic use.

We must, then, imagine the arrival in positions of power of men of Scandinavian taste in a society whose artistic activity was largely dominated by the Anglo-Saxon version of Germanic taste. Artists and craftsmen in historic times worked necessarily to the taste of their patrons because their very livelihood depended on pleasing those patrons. Only if their work was to an acceptable standard and style would they get paid.

Sir Thomas Kendrick, over half a century ago (Kendrick 1941), devoted an interesting essay to the problem of identifying Scandinavian taste in pre-Conquest England. He suggested that true Viking taste was seldom seen in England but that Viking love of animal-based art revived an interest in Anglo-Saxon animal art. Prior to the tenth century, he said, 'In the victorious West Saxon districts of England from which the Danes had been expelled, the Christian and quasi-Carolingian 'Winchester' art had been established, and for the leading men of free England Viking art was a hostile thing, representing heathendom and the abominable enemies of English civilisation; while inside the Danelaw the Viking settlers themselves struggled, presumably with no grander equipment than modest wood-carvings and minor metal and bone ornaments, against a magnificent and firmly established Hiberno-Saxon art that, expressed in an imposing series of sculptured crosses and illuminated books splendidly surpassed Viking art in its own idiom'.

He went on to suggest that most of the so-called Jellinge style animals in English carving are appreciably anglicized. (One of his two exceptions, however, comes within our scope, and we shall consider it shortly. This is the 'Bound Devil' at Kirkby Stephen.) So, too, he wrote, the great cross in the churchyard at Gosforth 'would have to be called Anglo-Norse, even if it did not bear Edda subjects'.

That this sort of remark could be used in such a 'throwaway' fashion over fifty years ago is not an accident. It results directly from the work of the two men. The first of these was the Rev W. S. Calverley, vicar of Aspatria. Originating from the area of Leeds, he came to Cumbria in 1872, when he was ordained

at Carlisle and became assistant curate of Eskdale. Further assistant curacies followed at Maryport and Dearham, where he took over as vicar in 1877. After eight years at Dearham he moved to Aspatria, and was still its vicar when he died in 1898.

A quarter of a century in Cumberland produced, from a man who suffered from heart disease for some years before his death, an astonishing series of papers, many of them dealing with subjects never before seriously studied. Because he made so significant a contribution to the study of pre-Conquest sculpture we tend to forget that he was also involved in work at Hardknott Roman fort and on Hadrian's Wall. But a long series of studies of carved stones illustrated by his own pencil drawings would have been his primary memorial were it not for a second remarkable man, W. G. Collingwood.

He was a Liverpool man whose name became inextricably linked with the Lake District, and he was, for the first thirty years or so of this century, the presiding genius of Cumbrian archaeology. At Oxford he had become acquainted with Ruskin and the school of William Morris. An artist himself, he became both Ruskin's secretary when Ruskin retired to Brantwood, and Professor of Fine Art at University College, Reading. His artistic skills and an interest in Norse matters, much fuelled by a visit to Iceland, led him to take on the completion of a book projected by Calverley before his death. This eventually emerged in 1899 as *Early Sculptured Crosses and Shrines in the Diocese of Carlisle* allegedly by Calverley and edited by Collingwood (Calverley (ed.Collingwood)1899). What the resemblance may be between this and the book Calverley might have produced alone we shall never know, but the book appears to be an early instance of what is described in Collingwood's obituary: 'Many of the articles [in the *Transactions* of the Cumberland and Westmorland Antiquarian and Archaeological Society] which he edited were completely rewritten by himself ...'.

This book, unencumbered by restrictions of date or culture in its title, described all the then known pieces of pre-Conquest sculpture in Cumberland and Westmorland, a number of demonstrably later pieces of carving, and several pieces of metalwork; and it even strayed outside its own professed geographical area occasionally. Of the 'Shrines' there was very little trace.

No such all-embracing coverage was carried out for the remainder of our region. Both G. F. Browne and J. Romilly Allen published articles dealing with sculpture in Lancashire and Cheshire, and thereby included Viking Age pieces; and by 1906, Henry Taylor's *Ancient Crosses and Holy Wells of Lancashire* had appeared in volume form and, to a certain extent, was a useful source book, though the greater part of the book was taken up with post-Conquest crosses and cross-bases, together with the holy wells, which form a rather curious additional subject.

It is, of course, a marvellous thing for scholarship that all the pre-Conquest sculpture of England is in the process of being fully described and illustrated in the *Corpus of Anglo-Saxon Stone Sculpture* being published under the aegis of the British Academy.[1] It should be noted, not as any form of criticism but as a matter of information, that the term 'Anglo-Saxon' in the title of the series subsumes such things as Viking Age. All sculpture likely to be of pre-Conquest date is dealt with.

A further point is that the illustration of the surviving sculpture itself is entirely by photography. This is not the place to argue the merits and demerits of this method, but we may note in passing that photography is not entirely objective, being dependent on such technicalities as lighting and purely photographic variables in exposure, developing and printing. Conversely, drawing is greatly subjective, but can, as Calverley and Collingwood showed, illuminate points which are difficult to make clear by photography.

As far as the area we are considering is concerned, a single volume of the *Corpus* covering Cumberland, Westmorland and Lancashire-north-of-Sands appeared in 1988 (Bailey and Cramp 1988). Reference to this volume, which is arranged alphabetically by site, will provide a description, discussion and illustrations for all the pieces about to be considered within that area. Further south, in the remainder of Lancashire and in Cheshire, as constituted prior to 1974, references are more scattered, and will be provided where necessary.

In beginning to look at the sculpture itself, we will be self indulgent and begin with the best. The superb cross standing in what is presumably its original base and original position within the churchyard at Gosforth (Cu) (figure 35) has attracted superlatives. It has been called the largest piece of pre-Conquest sculpture surviving in Britain, and probably merits the title. More important is the fact that the whole monument is but slightly damaged and the carving has survived a thousand years of West Cumberland weather with little obvious ill effect.

We may digress for a moment at this point to consider a subject often raised when early sculptures and weathering are discussed. This is the possible protection of the monument from further deterioration by, for example, placing it within the church concerned or other suitable building, with or without the provision of a replica on the original site. This subject is complex and has produced a considerable literature. The procedure has been carried out, as for example in the case of the great cross at Cashel in Co.Tipperary, and examples such as this will provide experimental data. In summary, however, it must be said that the apparently simple step is fraught with uncertainty. The monument concerned will, while outside, have achieved some kind of equilibrium with its environment, but, like any other piece of stone, carved or otherwise, it will have been subject to erosion. Alter that environment, and a different set of pressures

Figure 35. The Gosforth cross.

is created. Permanently drier conditions, normal within doors, and greater temperatures, again usual, may result in more rapid deterioration than was previously occurring. More closely controlled environments require some form of case, which is likely to be both expensive and unsympathetic. Thus to the simple suggestion, 'Why not bring it inside?' the answer may well be, 'It may be better off where it is'.

To return to the Gosforth Cross: it is made from the pinkish red sandstone so frequently found in West Cumbria, though its resistance to weathering suggests the use of a harder bed than was often used for medieval sculpture. Its base is a single stone cut with three steps. Whether or not it is necessary to cite resemblances to the cross on the rock of Golgotha in support, there is presumably no doubt that the generally pyramidal form of medieval cross-bases, both pre- and post-Conquest, is intended to recall Calvary. Above the base, the shaft of the cross, which consists of a single stone, is cylindrical and undecorated for some three feet or so. Passing upwards, there then ensues an area of the so-called 'ring-chain' pattern, which is produced by the carving in relief of 'Y'-shaped figures whose sides are all concave, each concavity receiving the stem of another 'Y' shape. At the top of this area, the cross-section of the shaft changes to rectangular by the carving of four downward curving mouldings a little like the facets produced when a circular pencil is sharpened with a knife. The resultant form – cylindrical stem merging upwards into rectangular shaft – was given the name 'staff-rood' by Collingwood, who saw a wooden prototype as its origin. The shape appears most frequently in an area centred on the Peak District, but variants are found in a number of sites in our present area.

All four sides of the rectangular portion are carved with relief decoration consisting of human and animal figures together with formalised 'dragons', to the significance of which we will return shortly. The whole monument is capped by a cross whose arms are nearly straight-sided and expand somewhat in width towards their ends. The arms are joined by a continuous stone ring, and there is a boss in the centre.

All the features which have been enumerated are more or less familiar in pre-Conquest sculpture, but all are at Gosforth slightly out of the ordinary in some way. The staff-rood form, as already indicated, is by no means a rarity, but no other has the slender proportions found here. The cross-head, too, is much smaller than would be expected, and the straightness of the outline of its arms is uncommon. The ring-head, of course, is found on many monuments, and is particularly widespread in Ireland. It has been pointed out that the ring is an unnatural form for stonecarving, and may well derive from a form of bracing for a wooden cross made up of four separate arms. The presence of bosses where arm and ring meet, though not found at Gosforth, is sometimes cited in favour of this origin for the ring.

Today we can go and look at the Gosforth Cross (prosaically 'Gosforth 1' in the *Corpus*), read the descriptions of it, and take its Scandinavian background for granted. It is salutary, therefore, to read a little of what Calverly wrote of it (Calverley (ed.Collingwood) 1899), and to relive a little the sense of discovery felt over a century ago. 'On the 8th of July, 1881, the Cumberland and Westmorland Antiquarian and Archaeological Society inspected the famous cross in Gosforth churchyard ... I expressed the thought that the sculptures on the panel on the west face indicated the binding to a rock of Loki ... Further study ... has resulted ... in what ... the Rev. G. F. Browne [called] "a *revelation* of the language of these stones which no one had dreamed of before".'

The process of that study included the cleaning of the cross, and it is fortunate that nothing was then done to equal the disasters which occurred on more than one occasion to the great Anglian cross at Bewcastle. 'I have', wrote Calverley (Calverley (ed. Collingwood) 1899, 140), 'a very vivid recollection of going to Gosforth one dull wet day in the late autumn of 1881, when I thought that the continuous damp and rain of the previous weeks would have softened the lichens which had filled every sculptured hollow on the crosshead, and of standing with Dr Parker beneath the cross, whilst his coachman, up aloft, with a dash of a wet brush to the right and to the left hand scatterd the softened mosses,[2] and revealed – what none had seen clearly perhaps for centuries – the sign of the ever-living Trinity, the triquetra of the Book of Kells and other MSS. of the early Christian church.'

Calverley went on to identify all the sculpture on the cross with people and scenes from Norse mythology. Slightly greater caution prevails today, though the general idea is undoubtedly correct. We may crystallize the difference between the views of the late nineteenth century and those of the late twentieth by saying that Calverley saw all the scenes as *purely* Norse. That is to say they were representations of figures and events described in known written versions of the Norse myths. He saw their *function* as Christian and didactic. 'As the four planes carrying the world-stories taper upwards towards the perfect circle with its centre and Holy Symbols, so the truths displayed thereon – Christian and Heathen – run side by side towards one Infinite Truth.' Thus he describes each face carefully, identifying Loki, Heimdal, Odin and others; but when he comes to the east face he says 'But who is *this* central figure on the *east side* of the cross?' and suggests Odin, Baldr or Heimdal 'or all the *three in one*' as his answer. Later he refers to a '*central Heimdal-Christ*' on the west face and a '*central Thor, Odin, or Baldr-Christ*' on the east face, and suggests that if 'the pagan Northern colonists of this coast' saw heathen scenes on the cross, 'the native British Christian' would see the Christian interpretation.

Calverley's identification of the scenes on the cross was undoubtedly broadly correct, but the pagan/Christian interpretation of them somewhat tortuous. Present day thinking tends to suggest a mixture of scenes, with the east face being a straight presentation of the crucifixion of Christ, even though that raises some iconographical difficulties. For example, although the lack of representation a cross itself is readily paralleled, the pairing of the spear-bearing soldier ('Longinus') not with a sponge-bearer ('Stephaton') but with a female figure is not so easily explained. It is thus suggested that, to quote Bailey in the *Corpus* (Bailey and Cramp 1988, 102), 'the Crucifixion (the end of one world and the beginning of a new) is set alongside – and by implication compared and contrasted with – the end of another world drawn from Scandinavian mythology.'

Collingwood reproduced Calverley's original paper describing his discoveries in full in his editing of Calverley's book (Calverley (ed.Collingwood)1899), commenting 'To bring it up to date would destroy its documentary interest' and referring to it as 'an essay which it is not too much to call epoch-making'. He added that the carvers of the Gosforth cross 'carved a cross ... without all the *arrière-pensée* or deep comparative philosophy of religion which we may be tempted to read into their work' and therein may lie a lesson for all of us.[3]

It is in no way surprising that after the publication of Calverley's paper on Gosforth (in the Cumberland and Westmorland Society's *Transactions*) (Calverley 1883) attempts were made by others to find similar analogies to explain otherwise enigmatic sculpture. One site at which this was done was Halton (La) where the base of a cross had apparently been left in position to support a sundial when the remainder of the cross was demolished in 1635. G. F. Browne had, in 1885 (Browne 1885), recognised parts of the saga of Sigurd on the cross at Leeds parish church. Browne, incidentally, appears in the literature

Figure 36. The lowest stone in the Halton cross (scale in inches).

variously as 'Canon', 'Professor' and 'Bishop'. He was, in fact, first (1887) Disney Professor of Archaeology at Cambridge, then Canon of St Paul's (1891) and, finally, Bishop, initially of Stepney (Suffragan, 1895) and then of Bristol (1897) until his retirement in 1914.

Six years after Browne's identification at Leeds, the scenes on the east face of the Halton fragment were identified also as showing part of the Sigurd story. Some uncertainty, however, surrounds the identity of the discoverer of that fact. Priority has usually been given to Dr Henry Colley March, who published a paper entitled 'The Pagan Christian Overlap in the North' in 1891 (March 1891). He included illustrations of a number of Norwegian stave church doorways which showed the Sigurd story, and these illustrations, not otherwise easy to come by, have been frequently copied. Collingwood, however, allowed his edition of Calverley's work to

stray outside the borders of the Diocese of Carlisle to Halton, partly, as he put it, to provide 'the justice due to an original investigator'. The Halton paper by Calverley which he reproduced was the then unpublished text of a lecture given to the Lancaster Philosophical Society in February, 1891. This recounted the visits made by Calverley to Halton in the summer and autumn of 1890 which presumably preceded Colley March's researches which resulted in his 1891 paper.

Today, the question of priority of discovery matters little. What is important is the presence at Halton of a cross fragment bearing what is probably the clearest representation of part of the Sigurd story outside Scandinavia.

Before we look at the stone itself, it may be as well to recount that part of the story of Sigurd the Volsung which appears in sculptural depictions. The story concerns one of the exploits of Sigurd, who is a Hero. At the moment which conerns us, he is dealing with two brothers, Regin and Fafnir, the former his foster-father. Regin has been in possession of a great treasure, which has been taken from him by his brother who has turned himself into a dragon, thereby making recovery of the treasure difficult otherwise than by the employment of a Hero. Regin, however, claims that he is no longer interested in the treasure but only in revenge, and that if Sigurd will kill Fafnir and recover the treasure, he (Sigurd) can have it.

Regin is a smith, craftsmen always regarded with awe in primitive societies for their ability to turn dull-looking ore or ingots into death-dealing weapons, which was thought of as potent magic. So, before Sigurd can accomplish his deed he must have a special sword. The first that is made is tried and breaks; the second parts a lock of hair floated onto its blade by a stream and is thus deemed satisfactory.

Sigurd may be a Hero, but he is neither foolhardy nor bound by rules of 'fair play'. Further, he is a good field naturalist. Before he attempts to outwit his dragon he observes its behaviour. The dragon, like many animals, is in the habit of going down to the water for an evening drink, so Sigurd's tactics are to dig a pit in the dragon's path, cover it with branches after hiding in it, and dispatch the dragon as he passes overhead. All goes well, and Fafnir duly pays for his evil deeds.

One of the passing advantages of killing dragons is that eating the flesh enables the diner to understand the language of the birds and the beasts. Accordingly, Sigurd impales the dragon's heart on a spit and roasts it. We have already seen that the great Hero has some engagingly human characteristics, and these include impatience, for he tries the roasting heart between his finger and thumb – and burns them. Just as you or I would, he pops them in his mouth, and in so doing absorbs enough of the dragon to hear and understand the voice of some birds in a tree above him, who are warning him that Regin is treacherous and is creeping up on him in order to kill him while his attention is distracted by matters culinary. Sigurd, wisely not far from his weapon, picks it up and removes Regin's head. This is as far as the story is taken at Halton and in most sculptural representations.

All of this is referred to, with the exception of the sword-trial, at Halton (figure 36) in two arched panels. In the lower Regin is seen working at his forge, hammering a sword blade held in pincers. The forge is blown by two prominent pairs of bellows. The hammer, the sword and the pincers are also shown separately. At the top of the panel is an interlaced knot representing Fafnir. The story then moves to the upper panel, where Sigurd is seen roasting Fafnir's heart on a spit above leaping flames, and sucking his burnt finger and thumb. The upper half of this panel has a stylized tree with the two warning birds. The last act of the story returns to the lower panel where is Regin's headless body with the head beside it.

It is quite easy, once the story is known, to recognise the elements of it in the carving. It would, however, have been impossible to derive the story from the carving alone, were it not known from literature. And herein lies the significance of its presence on this fragment of a Christian monument. While we could, with Collingwood's *arrière pensée*, devise allegorical meanings for the saga elements on the Gosforth cross, the Sigurd story as shown at Halton was simply a well-known and well-loved story, and the man who paid for the cross, with perhaps only a generation of Christianity behind him, saw no disrespect, no blasphemy and certainly no heathendom in having his favourite story alongside whichever Christian ones he chose for those parts of the cross now lost.

It has already been suggested that our ability to identify scenes carved on stone crosses and the like depends on some familiarity with the story on which the sculptor was working. The simpler the scene, the more important become any objects depicted alongside the figures. Ultimately, these 'attributes' became the chief means by which otherwise unidentifiable figures were differentiated, and they were codified for the identification of saints in medieval art. This idea had not yet taken root in the period with which we are dealing, however, and we have already seen that even a crucifixion scene, as at Gosforth, cannot certainly be identified as that of Christ as related in the Gospels.

It is, therefore, not surprising that a prominent attribute in a scene is seized upon in the public mind and identifies a figure. This has occurred at Kirkby Stephen (figure 37), where a stone bears a human figure held in ropes or some similar binding and has, close to its head, two curves or volutes which could be thought of as horns. From these features is derived the name of the Bound Devil (Bailey and Cramp 1988, no. 1, 120–121, illus. 390–393). In fact, although the description 'bound' cannot be argued with, the 'Devil' identification is by no means certain. The so-called 'horns' may or may not be intended to be attached to the head; and, in any case, the Devil's horns do not seem to be recorded with the curve downward. If, as seems posssible, the 'horns' are no more than a device to fill space, the bound figure may come from the sagas (Loki) or represent Christ struggling with evil. These are not the only possibilities, and we simply do not know. There are not enough attributes to tell us. It is worth making the comparison with the bound figure, usually agreed to be Christ, on the stone at Jelling.

Some sculptor at Kirkby Stephen had an original mind. Not only did he produce the extraordinary Bound Devil, but he fashioned another unique stone (Bailey and Cramp 1988, no. 3, 122–123, illus. 398–401). This is a piece of a shaft which is semi-cylindrical in cross-section and tapers, presumably upwards, towards a broadening which may have been part of a cross-head. The decoration of the fragment is unremarkable, but its shape is unparalleled, and it is quite possible that it is not part of a cross-shaft at all. There are

three or four other pieces from this period recorded from Kirkby Stephen, including one seen as recently as 1973 and now lost.

All the pieces we have so far discussed carry figure sculpture as well as non-figural decoration, and figure sculpture is always more interesting. The depiction of details of dress and decoration, if preserved, is always fascinating. There is, for example, a stone which, like the Kirkby Stephen one, has acquired a name. This is the 'Angel in Boots' (figure 38) from Slaidburn, which was first recorded in a wall and then lost, before resurfacing to end, at present, on display, somewhat irrelevantly, in Whalley Abbey. The attributes which led to the name are perfectly clear. It is a 'human' figure with wings – therefore it is an angel; and it wears boots with pointed toes and points before and after the opening. The stone is of the right proportions to have come from a cross-shaft, but nothing survives on the other faces to help us in further interpretation.

Figure 37. The 'Bound Devil' at Kirkby Stephen (scale in inches).

Figure 38. The 'angel in boots' from Slaidburn. Height 1′ 10″ (56 cm).

We have treated the Slaidburn stone as being from the Viking age, and indeed boots of the same type as those worn by the angel can be found on Scottish sculptures of about the right date for such assignation. It is, however, possible to demonstrate that this general tradition of stone-carving drawing on standardised emblems continued over several centuries, probably even beyond the date of the Norman Conquest, though uninfluenced artistically by that event. It has been widely suggested that the chevron-like element below the figure on the Kirkby Stephen 'Bound Devil' represents a feature seen elsewhere, for example at Whalley and at Bolton (La). Here the chevron can be seen to extend until it merges into the moulding which frames the cross, and it is suggested that this developed from the drooping, swag-like moulding which defined the transition from circular to square cross-section in staff-roods. This feature we have already seen at Gosforth, and, whatever the truth or otherwise of its development to the chevron arch, that feature itself can be seen not only in the places which we have already mentioned, but also in a sculpture which displays a figure wearing the same type of boots as seen at Slaidburn, combined with decorative features unlikely to be pre-Conquest.

To take things in order, we will look first at the Whalley cross, then that at Bolton, followed by the third one which consists of two stones now separated by some dozen miles and reunited in drawing form only. Convenience will then dictate that we return to Whalley to deal with the other two crosses in the churchyard there.

At Whalley, we have a situation somewhat different from that which we meet in many places where fragments of pre-Conquest sculpture are preserved. Often, these fragments represent the earliest surviving material remains of the Christian religion in the parish, and often, too, they are hidden in dark and dusty corners of the church, their carved faces in contact with stone cills or shelves, so that their decoration is eroded. At Whalley, though the crosses are not perhaps celebrated in the way that the Gosforth cross is (and it is not suggested that their decoration merits such fame) they are at least known, and known by name. Ask locally, and you will probably be referred to the 'Paulinus crosses'.

Thereby hangs a tale of some interest. The Whalley crosses were first brought to the notice of a wider audience than the local populace by Thomas Dunham Whitaker. He described, in his magisterial *History of ... the Ancient Parish of Whalley* (Whitaker 1800,33) how the Whalley crosses were first mentioned in writing, as far as we know. This happened in the early years of the fourteenth century, when the Cistercian monks of Stanlow Abbey (Ch) were in the process of removing to Whalley. There arose a dispute of which the details do not concern us, with the monks of the Cluniac Priory of Pontefract. As what we might now call a statement entered into court, the Whalley monks prepared a document known as *De Statu Blagbornshire.*

This might reasonably be translated 'The Situation in Blackburnshire' and is of considerable interest, though largely irrelevant to our present concerns. The monks, however, evidently considered that their case would be furthered by starting right at the beginning. They consequently stated that the church at Whalley had been founded by St Augustine, and cited as evidence of this antiquity the presence in its churchyard of '*lapideae tunc erecteae et vocatae a populo Cruces beati Augustini, quae sub eodem nomine usque hodie ibi durant*' (stones then erected popularly called Blessed Augustine's Crosses which remain under the same name to the present day).

Now Whitaker did not believe this story, claiming that the monks had a 'fond and thoughtless devotion' to Augustine. He was, however, unwilling to discard the whole story on this account, and retained it by the simple expedient of substituting Paulinus, who he knew had evangelised in Northumbria, for

Augustine who had not. Thus a monk's fiction (for it is unlikely that the author of *De Statu Blagbornshire* had any better information about seventh century Lancashire than we have) became altered and hallowed by the hand of a great nineteenth century historian.

It is easy to make fun of all this, but how was Whitaker to date the Whalley crosses? He did his best, comparing them to what he knew, from Leland, of a cross at Dewsbury which carried the name of Paulinus and which he therefore believed to date from his time. Today we know that the Dewsbury cross had been a memorial to the fact of Paulinus's preaching erected perhaps two centuries after the event.

The particular cross at Whalley which brought us to this discussion is the largest of the three there and stands nearest to the main south door of the church (figure 39). It now consists of three stones; a base stone, a large piece of the shaft and another stone which appears to be the top of the shaft and the lowest arm of the cross head. The whole monument now stands just over nine feet (2.75m) high, but a portion is missing between the two pieces of the shaft. The length of this portion is a matter of opinion for, although Collingwood (Collingwood 1927, 108, figure 132) treated the cross-shaft as though it tapered regularly from base to top, this is not the case, so a mathematical assessment cannot be made.

Figure 39. The largest cross at Whalley. Height overall, as standing, 9′ ½″ (275 cm).

The decoration of the cross consists largely of lush, deeply-carved whorls and spirals, though the north face carries a row of raised diamonds topped by pellets. Both broad faces (W & E) do have the chevron arch which may be represented on the Kirkby Stephen 'Bound Devil', but there are other oddities about the cross. First, there are two places on the west face where the curvilinear decoration gives way to straight lines, and triangular shapes are formed. More unusually, from about half way up the surviving lower portion of the shaft it assumes a much more complex cross-section than the usual rectangle. On the narrow sides the framing borders come together and continue upwards as a central spine. On the east face the borders kink inwards a few inches and continue flanked by a toothed moulding. On the west, however, one of the borders changes into a toothed moulding while the other simply narrows and has no teeth present.[4]

The base stone, which is of a somewhat different material from the rest of the cross, is dressed only roughly to shape, some small areas being left untouched, and the socket for the cross is surrounded by an incised toothed line.

Surprisingly, the illustration accompanying this account is the first time anything like an accurate drawing of this cross has been published. J. M. W. Turner drew it for the engraving in Whitaker's *Whalley*, along with the others, but he made no real attempt to draw what we would now regard as an accurate illustration. Almost all who followed have done worse, the honourable exception being John Palmer, a self-taught Manchester architect, who produced a lithograph, dedicated to Whitaker, 'to preserve to future ages an outline of this monument of antiquity ...' in 1821.

At Bolton we have a cross (figure 40) the real nature of which has been obscured by a number of unfortunate occurrences. Three fragments were recovered when the parish church was rebuilt c. 1870. They were placed,

together with some other interesting fragments, in a room in the tower, where Browne saw them in 1887. He recommended to the vicar that they should be 'once more united, and placed in some position where visitors ... might see the handiwork of their Christian forefathers' (Browne 1887, 11–12). Something like this was done in 1890, but a whole series of errors was committed in the process. Firstly, the head was restored with a lower arm nearly twice the length of those of the surviving transom. Secondly, the two shaft portions were placed one on top of the other and disagreements in the 'fit' of the decoration 'corrected' in cement. In particular, for our purpose, the top of the chevron arch was added and joined to a boss on the stone above it. Thirdly, the cross was erected so close to a wall that one side can now be examined only with the hand.

As if all this were not enough, the resulting structure was drawn and published by Romilly Allen (Allen 1894) as though it were a single piece of stone, no indication of breaks or restoration being given. Even the scale of Allen's drawing was wrongly indicated. Sad to say, illustrations of the restored cross perpetuating Allen's errors have appeared in print as recently as 1983.

The Bolton cross was a very simple one in terms of its decoration. Both the broad faces have simple knots carried out in broad straps. There was a boss near the top of one face, but it has lost its surface. On the other broad face the upper motif is a sort of rectilinear meander, while at the bottom, below the heavy moulding which surrounds the shaft towards the base, is a motif consisting of a ring crossed by two straps, saltire-wise, each of which ends in a small boss.

The narrow faces have rectilinear decoration, with one exception, one side being linked to Whalley in the appearance of raised diamonds, though without pellets. The decoration of both narrow sides continues onto the ends of the arms of the surviving part of the cross head, showing that it has at least been restored the correct way round. The faces of the cross-head have bosses on one side and spine-and-boss on the other.

What must, surely, be the final flowering of the tradition we have been following is represented by a cross which has been given the name Anderton/Hollowforth (figure 41) for reasons which will appear. Its recent story starts with the presence in the parish of Anderton (La) of a Scheduled Ancient Monument known as 'Headless Cross'. This consists of the lowest part of the shaft of a cross surmounted by a flat quadri-lateral stone which has served at times as the base for a sundial and as a direction post. We may ignore this stone, but that on which it rests is another matter. It is said to have been erected by the first Lord Leverhulme, who had at his Rivington bungalow, not far away, a collection of carved stones. We may note, however, that the name 'Headless Cross' is recorded in the eighteenth century.

The Anderton fragment bears a moulding near its base like that at Bolton. Below it on

Figure 40. The cross at Bolton. The head is a more probable restoration than that carried out at Bolton. It is probable that there was another piece of stone between the two shaft fragments. Height as reconstructed 5′ 10″ (178 cm).

Figure 41. The 'Anderton/Hollowforth' cross. A drawing reconstruction only; the lwer stone remains at Headless Cross and the upper is in the Harris Museum and Art Gallery, Preston. Height of remains as reconstructed 8′ 4″ (254 cm).

one narrow face is a rectilinear meander; the other is worn beyond recovery. Above the moulding on the narrow faces are, on one side, a Greek Key pattern and, on the other, a curvilinear symmetrical pattern, very worn. The decoration on the broad faces is less expected. One is divided into panels by broad raised straps. These produce diamond-shaped and triangular fields. Two of the diamonds have raised crosses within them, each bearing an incised cross. Four of the triangles carry raised broken-triangle designs.

The other broad face carries the real surprise, however, for it displays, above the moulding, the lower half of a human figure. Two aspects only of this figure are clear: it wears a skirt-like garment finishing above the knees, and it wears strikingly depicted footwear.

There this curiousity would have remained, unexplained, had not another stone been discovered in the garden of a house called Hollowforth, north of Preston – hence the name given to the complete monument. This house was much modified by Richard Threlfall (1804–1870) who, like Lord Leverhulme a century later, was a collector of carved stones. Among other things, he acquired the crocketted finials from Preston parish church at the time of its rebuilding, placing them on the house called Hollowforth, which he was responsible for converting, as one source has it, 'from a simple farmhouse to a delightful country residence'.

The stone which was found a few years ago in the garden of that house formed what was obviously the upper part of the shaft of which Headless Cross, Anderton, was the lower portion. The new stone explained one or two of the problems raised by the other, and added new information about the whole monument.

On the Greek Key narrow side, that decoration continued upwards for about the same distance, terminating in a moulding above which the decoration had almost all gone, though there was a hint of diagonal elements. On the other narrow side it was now clear that the decoration consisted of a medallion plant-scroll of decidedly archaic aspect. The remains of the same moulding as on the first narrow side terminated this,

though the moulding itself had gone. Above it was a spiral stem without buds or leaves.

On looking at the broad faces it was clear that the mouldings referred to on the narrow sides represented the ends of chevron arches not unlike those we have followed from Kirkby Stephen *via* Whalley and Bolton. Starting at the bottom of the second stone on the first broad face, however, the first diamond panel contained a plant stem with two volutes, a bud and a drooping trefoil head. Above this the panelling ended in a small chevron arch which itself terminated in a trefoil. In the somewhat oddly-shaped panel below it was a quatrefoil. The main chevron arch then carried on up the centre of the shaft as on the west face at Whalley.

On the main face, the remainder of the human figure was revealed. It was clearly naked from the waist upwards and the hands, clasped across the lower chest, held what appeared to be a cross, but was probably a sword. The head and upper chest of the figure were worn so smooth that it seemed clear that the fragment had lain flat in some position where it had been walked on in this part. The head of the figure was topped by what appeared to be a trefoil, fitting into the chevron arch. This, like the one on the reverse side, continued upwards as a central spine which soon branched sideways to give a cross-shaped area. In total contrast to the condition of the head of the figure a short distance below it, the cross-shaped area was rough and jagged, as though its decoration had been smashed off. Position and proportion make it seem very likely that this part of the shaft bore a crucifix. Above the cross-shaped area, in the upper quadrants of the possible crucifix, were diagonally placed quatrefoils. Nothing remained of the cross head itself, but the mouldings at the top of the broad sides suggest that it was much like that at Whalley.

Attempts to date eccentric monuments of the kind we have been considering are difficult and possibly futile. It would not be impossible, however, to see the Whalley cross in the eleventh century, possibly in its second half, and Anderton/Hollowforth as towards the end of that century. No Norman influence can be readily traced, but the trefoils and quatrefoils, particularly on the broad face without the figure, seem likely to be post-Conquest. Even here, caution must be expressed, for a layout not unlike that of the diamond panels, containing a number of otherwise unfamiliar plant forms, is known on a fragment of a cross at Collingham in the Wharfe valley, and another at Kirkby Wharfe is not dissimilar. These both have on their narrow sides Greek key decoration which is interestingly similar to that on Anderton/Hollowforth. Neither has anything like the figure, which recalls the later crosses in the Irish series, though the figure is somewhat different from the ecclesiastics familiarly found there. On the other hand there is no sign of the distinctively late features (pointed arch, acanthus) which serve to date the cross at Thrybergh in the Don valley. The diamond layout is also found on one of the two great crosses in the Market Place at Sandbach, (Ch.).

We were brought to this consideration of the Whalley, Bolton and Anderton/Hollowforth crosses as a side issue from looking at sculpture with figures. Before we return to that theme we might note that the derivation of what we have called the chevron arch from the mouldings on a staff-rood, first suggested by Baldwin Brown, is in no way proved. Other sources for it may yet be found. It is also worthy of thought that the stone-collecting propensities of Richard Threlfall, illustrated by the fact of his acquisition of the finials from Preston parish church, may suggest that the Anderton/Hollowforth stone may first have stood in Preston. It is now in the Harris Museum in that town.

Our pursuit of the chevron arch took us from Kirkby Stephen first to Whalley, where we considered a cross without figural subjects. We return there now because both the

other crosses in the churchyard at Whalley do carry figures, and interesting they prove to be. Before we describe them in detail, it may be as well to say something about their history. We have seen that the fourteenth century monks of the Cistercian Abbey attributed them to evangelism by St Augustine, and that neither the occurrence of that mission nor the attribution of the crosses to that period can be sustained. It is nevertheless very interesting that the monks stated that the crosses were known by the name of 'Blessed Augustine's crosses' at the time they were writing. Presumably such a statement relating to the then present day could hardly be untrue, and therefore a tradition of early date for some crosses in Whalley churchyard was already in existence.

We do not know for certain what vicissitudes the crosses now there may have sustained before they were described and illustrated by Whitaker at the very beginning of the nineteenth century. He himself said that they 'were laid prostrate, and in danger of being destroyed, at the induction of Mr Johnson [1738], whose first care it was to have them firmly and durably erected *upon their original bases*'. (my italics) However, there is another story, which is both more entertaining in its own right and concerns a much better known figure than Mr Johnson.

John Webster (1610–1682) was at one time Master of Clitheroe Free Grammar School, and was the author of *The Displaying of Supposed Witchcraft* (1677). The story of his involvement with the Whalley crosses is told by the nineteenth century editor of T. Potts's *Wonderful Discoveries of Witches in the Countie of Lancaster* (Crossley (ed.), 1845, xxxix). It is this account which recorded the story of the Pendle Witches, so beloved of romanticists and tourism promoters. Of Webster we are told: 'During the Usurpation he is said to have headed a party by whom the three crosses of Whalley were removed from their sites, and placed as a boundary fence for some adjoining fields. After the Restoration, when his religious views had become sobered, he is said to have purchased the crosses from the person who then possessed them and to have re-erected them on their present site at his own cost'.

This is a delightfully moral tale of sober repentance, and is not impossible to reconcile with the story of Mr Johnson. There was plenty of time, in the period of more than fifty years which passed between the Restoration and the induction of Mr Johnson, for the crosses to have fallen, especially if their re-erection under Webster had not been particularly carefully done. What is worth noting is that their present dispersed positions, which can be shown to date from at least the beginning of the nineteenth century, are unlikely to have been selected without prior conditioning factors.

We will now turn to the cross which lies furthest from the church, being some 54 feet south of the main door. It consists of a shaft (figure 42), cut from a single stone, slightly under eight feet high. It is in a number of ways closer to crosses of pure Anglo-Saxon date than most we shall be considering, and its cross-section, being nearer to a square and less slab-like, is the first of such characteristics. Its decoration, too, is laid out in panels which seem to be old-fashioned at the likely date of its carving, though the panels are created by leaving horizontal bands between decorative motifs and enclosing the whole in a single incised line.

The contents of the six panels which adorn the east face are as follows, beginning at the top: a twist, with complete rings surrounding the cross-overs; a bird; a standing human figure; a quadruped; a diagonal key pattern; and an interlace. The human figure is most interesting, and it is frustrating that detail which was probably once present has now gone. All that can really be said is that the figure faces the spectator, arms bent at the elbows and hands raised to the level of the chin. There is a hem line which shows the figure is clothed, the head is surmounted by

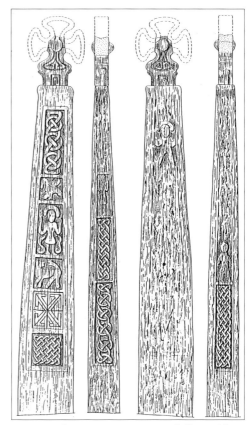

Figure 42. The westernmost cross at Whalley. Height of shaft only, 7' 10" (224 cm).

what represents either hair or a half-nimbus, and below the elbows appear two creatures which are probably serpents.

The scene as it stands cannot be certainly attributed to any known scene. It approaches the representations of Christ conquering evil as portrayed by one or more serpents, but they are normally beneath his feet. It has been suggested that it is an attempt to show Daniel in the Lions' Den (Bailey 1980, 159, figure 38,b.), but the quality of the depiction of the creatures above and below the scene makes it unlikely that even the exigencies of a narrow panel would cause such a sculptor to make lions look like serpents.

The bird above and the animal below are indeed well executed, and any uncertainty we have about their identity is probably due to erosion. The bird, its wings raised and its head and tail drooped, could be an eagle. The animal, with its backward-turned head and its tail raised over its body, does not closely recall any particular creature, though a number are possible. What we are really faced with, as so often, is an inability to know what was *meant* by a carving executed a thousand years ago.

If lack of detail on the east face makes the identification of its subjects almost impossible, the erosion of the stone makes even the mere observation of carving on the other three sides difficult. Nevertheless, it can indeed be observed under the right lighting conditions. The south face, then, has a long panel of interlace near its base, with a standing human figure in the panel above. This figure has its arms by its sides, but no other detail is discernible. The west side at a first glance yields nothing, but slowly moving shadows cast by bright winter sunshine revealed another figure almost at the top of the shaft. This figure, like all on this cross, is frontal, but has its legs splayed, and its arms, bent at the elbows, appear to grasp the frame of the panel. The hair/nimbus feature can also be discerned. Finally, on the north side, above a panel of twist and another of interlace, is the fourth figure, this time with hands raised and a garment hem, as on the east side, but with no other attributes recoverable.

The fact that the four figures, with their slight differences in pose still visible even if little else is, are carved in such a manner that the feet of the second are roughly level with the head of the first, and so on, passing anti-clockwise round the shaft from the south, must have had significance, but it eludes us today. The fragment of shaft and head now present on top of the shaft we have been considering almost certainly belonged to another monument.

That there were other monuments at Whalley is shown by the presence of at least two fragments built into the fabric of the church and two more from the site now in

Blackburn Museum. Yet another shaft is, however, present in the churchyard. This lies close to the priest's door, and is erected in a socket cut in a block of stone which carries half of a similar socket at its end. We can say, therefore, that there were probably at least two crosses side-by-side at Whalley, but whether or not they were pre-Conquest in date and whether or not any of the present three belonged in the socket stone we cannot say. We do know that there were later crosses at Whalley because the head of one has been placed on the third pre-Conquest shaft.

This shaft is also much worn (figure 43), and in a difficult spot for observation. It has also, at some time, been split or dressed so that only its west face (as at present) and half its north and south faces survive. Luckily the pattern on the north face is such that we can say that a little less than half the east-west

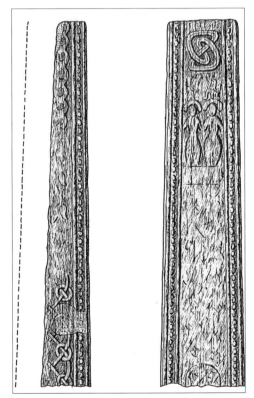

Figure 43. The easternmost cross at Whalley. Height surviving, 5′ 0″ (153 cm).

thickness of the shaft has been removed. Why this damage occurred is hinted at by the fact that a fragment of pink sandstone built into the south wall of the chancel probably comes from this shaft.

Its chief interest lies in the fact that again we have figures. This time there are two, side by side, and again we can discern little about them. Their arms are by their sides, they have the hair/nimbus feature, but they differ in outline from the others we have seen at Whalley. Their garments (presumably) mean that they are bulbous, almost insectlike, below the waist. We may recall in this connection that the tapestry of the seated Christ in Coventry Cathedral produces the same effect at a casual glance, and perhaps conclude that the Whalley figures are seated.

That Whalley was of some ecclesiastical importance in the late pre-Conquest period we can deduce not only from our cross-fragments but also from the fact that at Domesday the entire vill was held by the church, and from the vast size of its medieval parish. No such evidence exists for another place where the accidental survival of a single piece of stone hints at what we have lost elsewhere. This is at Winwick (La.), where, in the late eighteenth century, a very large piece of stone was used as a gravestone. The mason who smoothed the surface of part of it in order to carve his inscription did not, mercifully, remove more than was necessary, and we are left with the tantalising fragment of a monument which must have been the nearest thing in England, of which we have evidence, to an Irish High Cross.

Its size is determined by the fact that what exists is the transom or horizontal arm of the cross, and this is five feet in length. It is carved on one side (we will call it the front) with a central boss containing four interlaced triquetras. Above this is a zone of diagonal key patterns which show signs of being cleverly managed to fit in the shape produced by the part-circular 'armpits' of the cross. Below the boss is a zone of running Stafford

knots. The face of each arm also has a zone of each of the motifs mentioned, but oddly they are near alike in layout instead of being mirror images, as one might expect. Even then there are differences, there being three diagonal key patterns on the sinister arm and four and a half on the dexter.

On the reverse, the central boss and another on one arm have been dressed smooth. The other arm is that which bears the eighteenth-century funerary inscription. The central boss was surrounded by interconnected 'C' shapes, while the arm bears three quadrupeds of which little detail survives.

The cross was a ring-head, and the underside of the arms, as often in Ireland, was carved, in each case with a diagonal pattern. The greatest interest of the fragment, however, lies in the carving of the ends of the arms. On one is a depiction of a man being held upside down by two others, who are sawing him in half vertically with a bow-saw. This Bailey has brilliantly demonstrated to be a depiction of the apocryphal martyrdom of Isaiah. On the other arm-end there is a single figure, who has reasonably been identified as an ecclesiastic from the additional presence of two crosses and a small structure which may well be a church or a shrine. This figure carries two objects with loop handles which have been identified as buckets or bells. That the latter are to be preferred is suggested by the presence, on the Bayeux Tapestry, below Westminster Abbey in the scene of the funeral of Edward the Confessor, of two men each carrying two handbells. One or two of the elements of the decoration of the Winwick cross are found on the cross at Dupplin, in Perthshire. These include the 'C' patterns, the diagonal key and the presence of decoration on the underside of the arms. Too much should not be read into these connections. The Dupplin cross is not a ring-head and the shape of the head is very different.

The Crucifixion apart, we have not yet been able to identify a scene from the Bible on any of our cross fragments. To do this, we must travel to Dacre (Cu.)(Bailey 1977). Here, we have part of a cross-shaft which has plaits on its narrow sides, one of its broad sides dressed off, and the type of scene we seek among the decoration of the remaining broad face. Here, there are in fact four scenes, and these, from top to bottom of the surviving fragment, are: a quadruped, interestingly with its head turned back, as at Whalley; a scene with two human figures; a representation of a hound jumping on the back of a stag (the hart and hound motif); and a scene with two figures separated by a rendering of a tree. The latter scene, not surprisingly, turns out to be the Temptation in the Garden of Eden. This can be called unsurprising only in the sense that a scene with a tree, two figures and a snake is likely thus to be identified. It *is* surprising in the sense that depictions of the Temptation in sculpture of this date are very rare in England and Wales. So, too, is the scene at the top of the shaft, which is the Sacrifice of Isaac. Both of the events in the Bible are obviously key points in the Christian message, but, although not uncommon in manuscript illustrations, they are much rarer in English sculptural tradition. The hart and hound which occupy the centre of the Dacre shaft could readily be interpreted as relating to one of a number of hunting scenes in pagan mythology. Placed between the two Christian scenes already described, they seem more likely to have a Christian significance, and an attack by evil (represented, perhaps, by a wolf rather than a hound) on a Christian soul may be thought more likely.

The motif, whatever its exact significance, does occur elsewhere among the sculpture we are considering, at Lancaster, (La.) among the cross fragments recovered from the north wall of the parish church in 1906, and among the decoration of the hogback at Heysham, to which we will return when we consider that particular class of monument. The Lancaster shaft has the hart and hound at the top surrounded by various zoomorphic and plant interlacings, while the lower half of the shaft

is occupied by a ring-knot which is closely matched by that on a shaft fragment built into the wall of the vestry at Melling (La.) in the Lune valley. Here, the narrow side of the shaft carries the remains of a ring chain pattern. Other ring-knots of similar type are to be found at Aspatria (Cu.) and Bromfield (Cu.), and, in a somewhat simpler version, at Great Urswick (La.).

It is not possible, or even useful, to try to mention every fragment of Viking Age sculpture in a survey such as this. Nevertheless, there are one or two more pieces with figures which seem worthy of mention, and, thereafter, two or three other groups of stones which deserve some attention.

Among the remaining figure sculpture, mention must be made of the Giant's Thumb at Penrith (Cu.)(Collingwod 1920). Here we have the inevitable result of close on a thousand years of erosion on a sculpture of soft red sandstone. Good evidence has recently been adduced that detail on many sculptures which was visible when the earliest photographic records were made is now disappearing at a greater rate than can have been possible in the past. Atmospheric pollution, and particularly 'acid rain', are blamed. It is quite certain that current photographic records of crosses such as this at Penrith show little more than a shape which might have been produced by the action of water on gingerbread. Nevertheless, Collingwood was able, in the early years of the century, to recover the details of a crucifixion scene, complete with representations of sun and moon as in many early depictions.

The mention of Penrith, to which we shall also return when we deal with hogbacks, prompts discussion of one of the most exciting of recent discoveries in the field with which we are dealing. This is the so-called 'Penrith Plaque' (Bailey and Cramp 1988, no. 11, 140–142, Illus. 524–531). It consists of a piece of limestone about a foot square bearing a crucifixion scene with certain peculiarities which make it particularly interesting. Its origin is not totally certain, since it emerged to general knowledge in a London saleroom. There is, however, good reason to believe that it was once in a collection at Lowther Castle and that its place of origin was Penrith. What makes it so interesting are the details of the crucifixion itself.

There is, for instance, no cross visible. Figures of the two Roman soldiers ('Stephaton' and 'Longinus') are shown, and Longinus's sponge appears in a cup shape. Details of Christ's garment and the forked shape of his beard are all nearly unknown, both in sculpture and in manuscript illustration, this side of the Irish Sea. By contrast, parallels abound in sculpture and metalwork in Ireland and, in a single example, in the Isle of Man. Without pursuing the precise iconographic and dating criteria, we can say that a very good case has been made for dating the Penrith plaque to our period. In particular, the shape of the hem of Christ's garment, drooping from the knees to corners right and left, has been likened to the same feature at Gosforth, and has led to the suggestion that some exemplar, perhaps deriving from Ireland, was available in Cumbria to be interpreted differently by the Gosforth and Penrith sculptors.

Whatever the antecedents of the Penrith plaque, it is a fairly sophisticated piece of carving. Some of the remaining pieces from the period which bear figure sculpture are much less so. For example, let us look at the case of Burton in Kendal (We). (Bailey and Cramp 1988, no. 1, 82–83, illus. 180–183). Here we have a cross shaft bearing, on one of its broad sides, a figure carrying two wands or sceptres over its shoulders and standing or treading on a serpent. It is presumably a representation of Christ triumphing over evil. Above this, two small figures flank what appears to be an empty cross. Again presumably, they are Mary and John, and the scene implies the Resurrection, which, after all, is a rather difficult subject to illustrate. The remaining sides of the shaft have twists, rings, interlace and key patterns, all quite competently carved. But the standard of the drawing of the figures shows how far down the road we have come from the best of Viking period sculpture. In addition to another fragment of what was probably a very similar shaft, there is at Burton a piece (Bailey and Cramp 1988, no. 3, 83, illus. 189–192) which shows what happened when attempts were made, by sculptors who had neither the artistic nor sculptural skills necessary, to continue the tradition. This piece has, on its most ambitious side, a series of meandering parallel lines which give the first impression of interlace. The remaining sides have only parallel zig-zag lines which really do little more than fill the space. The whole is held together visually by cable mouldings along the edges.

If the Burton in Kendal sculptures show us both artistic and technical skills declining, there are still one or two pieces to be considered where the process has not proceeded so far. One such site is Neston (Ch.), in the Wirral (White 1986). Here are two fragments which have been treated as belonging to a single cross, though there is no certainty that this is the case. The shaft tapers rather rapidly towards the top and belongs to a form which is well seen in a number of fragments at St John's Church, Chester. These suggest that the head, which does not survive at Neston, would have had a prominent ring, the arms represented only by lugs protruding from the ring, and the spaces between arms and ring not pierced but merely recessed. What is particularly interesting about the Neston pieces is the figures. These are: first, a priest, apparently in mass vestments. He is shown full-face and has a moustache and beard. His hands are raised, one holding a chalice, the other now broken away. From the left wrist hangs an object which has been variously interpreted. It has a strap, and has been thought to be a satchel for holding a book, specifically a gospel book, for which Irish parallels can be quoted. The most recent work, however, suggests that the 'satchel', which appears to be divided vertically, is the tasseled ends of a maniple.

Elsewhere on the stone are interlace, twists and rings, step patterns and cable-moulded borders, together with two other figure scenes. One clearly features an angel, shown full-face, with wings. The other is of a fight between two figures. Interpretations of this vary, depending on whether or not the figures are seen as having knives in their hands. If they do not, they may be Jacob and the angel, though no sign seems to exist of any distinction between the two. If they fight with daggers, no obvious identification of the scene appears to present itself.

Interestingly, another fragment of what seems to be a similar cross has recently been removed from the fabric of the church, and it, too, carries a fight scene, though this time the participants fight on horseback. Also on this stone are a stag being attacked by an animal (not quite the conventional hart and hound); a figure with a spear who may or may not be connected with the hunting scene; and the lower halves of two more figures. These two crosses, combined with other fragments, make Neston a most intriguing site.

A brief survey such as this cannot mention every fragment of sculpture of this period in our area. Nevertheless, there are at least four other pieces and a couple of groups of carving to which we must refer before we deal with a whole class of monument which we have so far ignored – the hogback.

First of the pieces which must be mentioned in their own right, then, is the shaft fragment from Great Clifton (Cu.). Removed from the fabric of the church at the beginning of the century, it merits our attention at this point because, although it does have human figures, they are completely subordinate to a number of rather splendid dragons, or, as they are known prosaically to specialists, 'ribbon beasts'. Such creatures occur perhaps less commonly among the sculpture we are considering than the popular imagination might suggest. On the main face of this shaft there

are at least five animals involved (the *mot juste*) in the decoration. In two cases they are being ridden by diminutive human figures, and at the base is a human figure with hair/halo and a skirt-like garment. This figure is enmeshed in interlacings which may be serpents. All of this was described by R. M. Lidbetter shortly after its discovery (Lidbetter 1902), and there are points in his brief paper which make one regret that this was his sole contribution to the Cumberland and Westmorland Society's *Transactions*. For example, he describes one of the beasts as 'a wolf-headed creature possessing a cunning and vindictive eye, suggestive of a cruel nature' and he adds 'As regards symbolism perhaps the less said the better', though he proceeds to disregard his own advice. His, too, must have been one of the earlier papers to have a scale in metric as well as Imperial measures to its illustrations.

A further point which is made in relation to the Great Clifton stone is that it is cut from beds of differing colour sandstone. The white and pink areas on this, as on one or two other pieces, seem to be unrelated to the decoration, which reminds us that it is certain that some, and probable that all, such sculptures were painted. Traces of colour are occasionally found, and, in museums, reproductions exist which use the types of colours found in manuscripts and these show how very different the monuments would have looked from their present appearance.

Dragons and other mythical beasts occur, of course, on other stones than that at Great Clifton. At Cross Canonby (Cu.) the cross-fragment is interesting in this context, but we ought not to leave the subject of representations of animals and figures without reference to one of the comparatively few stones within our scope which does not seem to have been part of a cross. This is the so-called 'Fishing Stone' at Gosforth (Bailey and Cramp 1988, no. 6, 108–109, illus. 332). It is now built into the interior of the church, and only one of its faces is visible. It was found, face down, in the churchyard in 1882, and its original function is not certain. It is too wide to have come from a cross like that in the churchyard, although that seems not to have been alone, for parts of two similar crossheads are in the church. A case has been made out for almost all the surviving sculpture at Gosforth having been the work of one person, and it seems more likely that the Fishing Stone was part of something like an architectural frieze.

At least the subject matter of the main scene is undoubted. What appears is a boat, with two men seated in it, facing the spectator. The boat is alike at bow and stern, and has a mast, apparently stumpy, amidships. The mast has an expansion at its upper end, and is a near-unique representation of a Viking ship in sculpture in the British Isles. The man on the spectator's right holds the endpost of the boat with his left hand and brandishes an axe with his right. The other figure holds what must be a fishing line in his left hand and what is probably a hammer in his right. The line passes behind the boat and below it to end among four fishes.

What we cannot see so clearly are the bait and the quarry. The former is, in fact, an ox-head and the latter no less than the World Serpent, Midgard. The fisherman, identified by his attribute of the hammer, is, of course, the god Thor, and his companion is the giant Hymir, holding the axe with which he cut the line when the expedition nearly became too successful for its own good. Above the fishing scene is a very fleshy plait which might well have had an animal head like those on the great cross, since the Fishing Stone has been somewhat pared down. Above again, and separated by a straight horizontal moulding, is a stag with its head turned back, its front legs enmeshed in a snake and its tail ending in a knot. The Hart and the Snake, the Christian soul and Evil, are straightforward interpretations of this. In the fishing scene, a non-Christian god also encounters evil in the form of a serpent. It is a matter of personal

opinion to decide whether or not these, like the crucifixion scenes on the churchyard cross, represent the same idea seen by Christian and non-Christian eyes, and, if so, what this implies.

Perhaps one of the most elegant of the depictions of a natural phenomenon which we have not mentioned is the cross at Dearham (Cu.) (Calverley (ed.Collingwood) 1899, 124–125). This is a ring-headed cross of the type mentioned at Chester in connection with the stones at Neston. That is to say that the ring, instead of simply joining the arms, as for instance at Gosforth, is the most prominent part of the head, and is closer to the spectator than the cross-arms, which are recessed, and disappear into the ring to emerge as lugs beyond it. In Cumbrian examples such as this, the spaces between the arms are fully pierced and not merely recessed as at Chester.

The decoration on the main face of the Dearham cross consists mostly of ring-chain like the lowest register of the Gosforth cross, but it all grows from what looks a little like a very large leek spreading into two stems as it ascends. This may well have been at or near ground level originally, as it certainly was when Calverley drew it in the churchyard. Today, on a plinth in the church with the whole of the 'bulb' exposed and a bare area below it, the effect is somewhat lost. This stem and the ring-chain area have been interpreted as the World-Ash Yggdrasil of Norse mythology. Be this as it may, there would, I suspect, be relatively few people who would describe its carving, the remainder of the surface being covered with plaits, spirals and knots, as Collingwod did as 'midway between the early laboriousness of Bewcastle and the coarse decadence of Halton'.

One final point in connection with this cross is that, on the reverse face to the possible World Ash is a line of four rectangular panels with saltires. This was at ground level when Calverley drew it and it is at just such a level that the 'tree' grows out of the ground.

We pass now to a word or two about two groups of sculpture rather than individual stones. The first of these is the 'school' identified by Bailey as the Cumbrian Spiral Scroll (Bailey and Cramp 1988, 33–38) school. The work of this school has been identified at fifteen sites, one an outlier at Addingham (Cu.) in the Eden valley, the remainder all in the Cumbrian coastal plain south of Aspatria. The traits which identify the school are: first, as its name suggests, a form of spiral scroll; next, the so-called 'stopped plait', in which the ribbon of a plait stops short before reaching the point at which it would have crossed another, instead of clearly passing over or under it; and, third (and less frequent because cross-heads are less often preserved), a particular form of head pattern. What the identification of this 'school' of sculpture means in terms of the organisation of the process of stone carving we do not know.

Another, smaller, group of carvings with unique characteristics has also been isolated (Bailey and Cramp 1988, 38–40) at Beckermet St John, Haile, Workington and Brigham (all Cu.), and close relationships have been demonstrated over longer distances with crosses at Aspatria and Bromfield (both Cu.) in north Cumbria and Lancaster and Melling (both La.) in the Lune valley.

Yet another small group of carvings which deserve our attention is of those which Collingwood named (Collingwood 1927, 90–93) the hammerheads. In these crosses the upper and lower arms of the cross are expanded to the same width as the transverse arms. There are good examples at Carlisle (Cu.) and (with a ring) at Addingham (Cu.) in the Eden valley. It is interesting to note that a cross of this type is depicted on each side of a slab from Kilmorie (now at Kirkcolm) in Wigtownshire. Depictions in relief of various forms of standing cross do occur on slabs occasionally, and attention is drawn to the Kilmorie slab (where both crosses are decorated) because there occurs a depiction of just such a cross, though totally plain, on a slab at Heysham (La.)(figure 44). This is interesting because Heysham has sculpture of both Anglian and Viking periods (the latter in the form of a hogback) together with a pair of pre-Conquest churches, the burial ground of one of which at least seems likely to have been in use in the Viking period (Potter and Andrews 1994, 122–124).

Our survey, then, has brought us round to Heysham, where our attention will be concentrated on the hogback, and we must, therefore, deal with this clearly defined class of monument. The precise reasons for the erection of stone crosses, whether in Anglian, Norse, Irish Early Christian or later medieval contexts, are much argued. Two things at least are certain. The first is that no single explanation covers all. Some we know to be funerary because their inscriptions tell us so, or at least ask us to pray for the souls of named persons. It does not, of course, follow that even these were erected either immediately after the death of the person named, or at or near his place of burial. Only a statement such as that on the lead cross seen by Camden, allegedly dug up at Glastonbury and recording the burial place of Arthur, could do this.

The motives for the erection of crosses, then, are various. By contrast, it is assumed that the hogback is a grave monument, and that it lay along the grave. Its shape accords well with this idea, but rarely does any evidence survive to support this. The Heysham example is such a rare case, for a skeleton and an iron spear were said to have been found under it in the early nineteenth century.

A case has been made out for the development of the hogback from earlier, house-shaped shrines, such as that surviving at Peterborough or represented by parts at Jedburgh. If this is true, the process parallels the enthusiastic adoption by the Norse of the stone cross on their arrival in these islands. Be that as it may, the hogback is a fairly distinctive monument. It is normally rectangular or bow-sided in plan and has more or

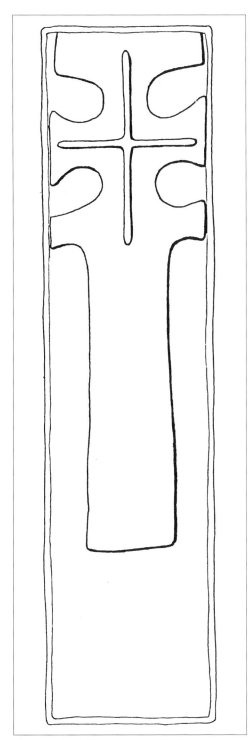

Figure 44. Cross-slab at Heysham showing a 'hammerhead' cross. Length 6′ 0″ (183 cm).

less vertical sides which come together rapidly towards the ridge, which, as the name suggests, is often convex. None of these characteristics is absolute, and examples breach them all, particularly in peripheral areas. They are found mainly in northern Britain, extending into Scotland, with a single example only in Ireland.

The commonest analogy for the shape of the hogback is that of a house, and parallels have been drawn with the shape of the houses at such sites as Trelleborg in Jutland. It is as a result of this analogy that the patterns on the 'roofs' of hogbacks are usually referred to as 'tegulae' – tiles – though the resemblance is sometimes minimal. Most curious of the features often found on hogbacks are the muzzled bears which clasp the ends of some of them. Collingwood noted the naturalism of these bears and contrasted it with the lack of naturalism in the portrayal of most animals at the time. He ascribed the presence of the bears to artistic genius, which obeys no rules, and of course it is true that we can almost never be sure how much we owe in a particular manifestation of an art style to the activities of an individual.

Within our area there are some twenty hogbacks of which at least part remains, and they occur at fourteen sites. In alphabetical order these are: Addingham (Cu.), Appleby (We.), Aspatria (Cu.), Bolton-le-Sands (La.), Brigham (Cu), Bromfield (Cu.), Cross Canonby (Cu.), Gosforth (Cu.), Heysham (La.), Kirkby Stephen (We.), Lowther (We.), Penrith (Cu.), Plumbland (Cu.) and West Kirby (Ch.). Of these sites three have more than one example, there being two at Gosforth, three at Lowther and four at Penrith. Not all require much comment here, but it is worth noting that several are, or have been incorporated in the fabric of later church buildings.

For example, that at Appleby St Michael, Bondgate Without (We.), is still in position as the lintel of a blocked west door of this now disused church. Its outer surface is flaking badly, and indeed has lost almost all of its decoration. The two Gosforth examples were recovered from the foundations of the church around the turn of the century; but perhaps the most interesting illustration of re-use is to be found at Plumbland (Cu.), where two pieces of a hogback are in the churchyard. One of them is carved to form a very good Early English corbel supported by a nice palmate stiff leaf. The fragment at Bolton-le-Sands (La.) is no more than a rectangular stone with remains of the hogback tegulation on one side, and it was therefore presumably used as a building stone. At what stage the face opposite to the tegulation acquired its carving of a figure and a snake is not known.

The shapes of hogbacks and the nature of their tegulation have, along with shapes and decoration of almost all other pre-Conquest carving, been classified (Bailey and Cramp 1988, xix–xxi), but there are too many variants and too few examples of any to make this classification very useful in north west England, at least in the case of hogbacks. Six of the ten shapes are represented, six of the ten varieties of tegulation, and six of the twenty hogbacks have evidence of end beasts.

What does seem to be clear as a regional idiosyncracy is a greater tendency to have figural scenes than in most areas. Particularly interesting in this respect are the two Gosforth hogbacks, two of those at Lowther and the Heysham example.

The Gosforth hogbacks have acquired the names of the 'Warrior's Tomb' and the 'Saint's Tomb', the first because of the battle scene on one of its sides, the latter because of the crucifixions on its ends. In shape they are somewhat different, the one being made up almost entirely of curves while the latter is straight edged. 'The Warrior's Tomb', with its battle scene, has been identified as the only surviving stone at Gosforth not to have been carved by the master mason whose work is represented at its best by the churhyard cross.

At Lowther (We.) we have on another hogback the only other contemporary representation of a Viking ship in English sculpture (figure 45) apart from that we have mentioned on the Fishing Stone at Gosforth. This example recalls some of those on the picture stones of Gotland in that its gunwale is lined by the round shields of the warriors who man it. Below the ship is a fish, and below that again what may be a sea-serpent. This runs the whole length of that side of the hogback, while above an enigmatic figure separates the ship from what appears to be an army of round-shielded warriors (? the ship's company again). Otherwise we have here what has been alluded to at Gosforth as a battle scene, but it is really a confrontation.

Oddly enough, hardly any of the sculpture on the hogbacks can be interpreted even with the degree of uncertainty which can be applied to the scenes on crosses. One is

Figure 45. W.G. Collingwood's 1906 drawing of one of the hogbacks at Lowther. (From Collingwood 1906).

Figure 46. The Heysham hogback.

reminded of the difference between the scenes, often biblical, on the Irish crosses and those with animals, warriors and horses on the bases of some of those crosses.

The Heysham hogback fits this pattern precisely (figure 46). What is actually depicted is clear, which is not the case on most of the other figured hogbacks. On one side, below some rather rudimentary tegulation, indicated by zig-zag lines, is a human figure with its hands raised, the figure being placed centrally and frontally to the viewer. To the spectator's left is a tree with a bird either side of it and one or more quadrupeds yet further to the left. Two quadrupeds, one facing either way, are to the right of the central figure.

On the reverse, the lower part of the tegulation is replaced by a quadruped, a horizontal human figure, some step patterning and a snake-like twist. Below this, two human figures with hands raised are at each end with half a dozen quadrupeds between them. One of these is certainly a stag, while two others might be dogs. Two more have very long tails held over their backs and doubled back, while the last animal is upside

down. This, like that below the tegulation, has a small curled tail, as does one of the ?dogs. Could they be boars?

Whatever they are, neither they, nor the other creatures on the stone, seem to have any particular relation to any other, and the same applies to the human figures. They might be in the *orans* praying position, but that is less than certain. Despite a number of attempts to 'explain' the sculptures, none has yet been put forward which is really convincing, and it has to go down as a 'don't know'.

Discussion of hogbacks takes us to the site which has the largest number of these in north west England – Penrith. Here, in the churchyard, is that peculiar 'monument' known as the Giant's Grave. It is not known at what date the six sculptured stones (two crosses and four hogbacks) which make up this feature were arranged in their present relationship, but it was certainly by the end of the seventeenth century, when they were drawn by Sir William Dugdale. It seems that their existence, or at least that of the two crosses, was recorded at the end of the sixteenth century, but that at that date they were no further apart than a normal grave. The architect in charge of the restoration of the monument at the end of the nineteenth century considered that there might have been two crosses, each at the western end of a grave, each grave in turn having two hog-backs upon it. After this, the cross between the two graves might have been moved to the opposite end of its grave, thereby spreading them as much as fifteen feet apart. This he supported on the grounds that the western cross was in its original socket, while the eastern was not; and that modern accumulation underlay the hogbacks, with willow pattern pottery found as deep as seven feet below the surface. This careful argument he then vitiated by suggesting that the whole 'monument' (except the western cross) was moved when the church was rebuilt in 1720. At least the story, apparently recorded in the late seventeenth century, that 'the grave' was opened, probably in the early seventeenth century, and that bones and a sword were found under it, seems to suggest that the 'grave' was of normal length and that it was not at that time encumbered by two or more hogbacks. Gibson, editing Camden's *Britannia* for republication in 1695, may be the originator of the 'Giant'.

Whatever the truth of the details of their movements, we can be quite sure that the present arrangement of the two crosses and the four hogbacks is of relatively recent origin. Whether or not the crosses were funerary in origin, the hogbacks clearly were, and each will have marked its own grave.

Our survey of the sculpture surviving in the four ancient counties of Cumberland, Westmorland, Lancashire and Cheshire, and likely to have been created during what we can loosely call the Viking Age, has been wide-ranging, but inevitably incomplete. There are great cross-shafts which we have passed by – at Muncaster (Cu.), Waber-thwaite (Cu.), Walton on the Hill (La.) – and many smaller fragments, which, together, serve to remind us that, although our notions of the appearance of the landscape and its buildings at the time we are considering may be somewhat hazy, one ubiquitous element in it will have been stone sculpture.

Notes

1. *The British Academy Corpus of Anglo-Saxon Stone Sculpture in England*, Oxford. Further volumes will ultimately cover Lancashire and Cheshire. Meanwhile several of the stones in those counties are discussed in Bailey 1996b.

2. Those familiar with ancient stones in exposed situations will know that, while 'a dash of a wet brush' might well have 'scattered the ... mosses', it is unlikely to have affected the lichens mentioned earlier in the sentence.

3. Bailey has, of course, convincingly drawn our attention (Bailey 1996a) to the way in which figural scenes on much Anglo-Saxon sculpture yield layers of meaning when viewed from the point of view of, and with the biblical and patristic background of, their monastic originators, but the fact that much sculpture of the Viking age cannot be connected in the same way with monastic activity suggests that Collingwood's point about the lack of *arrière pensée* in the conception of the Gosforth Cross at least may be correct.

4. Attention should be drawn to Bailey's suggestions, using, *inter alia*, this cross, that many such monuments had painted surfaces, metallic attachments, and/or were designed to look like metalwork (Bailey 1996 *passim*, particularly 38ff.).

References

Sir Mortimer Wheeler once wrote, in typical style, 'This is not a book for which an infinitude of footnotes is an apt harassment', and I initially inclined to his view. Wiser counsel, however, prevailed, and references, which I hope will be a helping hand rather than a harassment, have been provided. Readers unfamiliar with the wider background against which this book must be set will find numerous general works on the Vikings in every library. Appended are the details of a very short selection of such works which may help. Such a selection is always a matter of personal choice, and I am as conscious that other books clamour for inclusion as I am that some more specific publications might well have found a place among the References. The Further Reading list also includes details of the place-name volumes for each of the counties covered, so that those who wish to follow up an aspect of study of the settlement of the Norse not here dealt with may do so.
(Place of publication is London unless otherwise stated.)

Allen, J.R., 1894, 'The early Christian monuments of Lancashire and Cheshire', HSLC 45, 1–32a.

Bailey, R.N., 1977, 'The meaning of the Viking-age shaft at Dacre', CW$_2$77,61–74.

——, 1980, *Viking Age Sculpture in Northern England.*

——, 1996a, *Ambiguous birds and beasts: three sculptural puzzles in south-west Scotland*, (Fourth Whithorn Lecture), Whithorn.

——, 1996b, 'What mean these stones? Some aspects of pre-Norman sculpture in Cheshire and Lancashire', *Bull. John Rylands Univ. Lib. of Manchester*, 78, 21–46.

—— and Cramp, R.J., 1988, *Corpus of Anglo-Saxon stone sculpture in England*, Vol. 2, *Cumberland, Westmorland and Lancashire North-of-Sands*, Oxford.

Baines, E., 1836, *The History of the County Palatine and Duchy of Lancaster*, 4 vols, London, Paris and New York.

Baldwin, J.R. and Whyte, I.D., (eds) 1985, *The Scandinavians in Cumbria*, Edinburgh.

Birley, E.B., 1964, 'The Orton Scar Find', CW$_2$64, 81–89.

Blackburn, M.A.S. (ed.), 1986, *Anglo-Saxon monetary history: essays in memory of R.H.M. Dolley*, Leicester.

—— and Pagan, H., 1986, 'A revised check-list of coin-hoards from the British Isles, *c.* 500–1100', 291–313 in Blakburn (ed.) 1986.

Blunt, C.E., 1974, 'The Scotby Hoard', BNJ 42, 156–157.

Boe, J., 1932, 'An Anglo-Saxon bronze mount from Norway', *Ant.Jnl.* 12, 440–442.

Browne, G.F., 1885, 'The ancient sculptured shaft in the parish church at Leeds', JBAA 41, 131–143.

——, 1887, 'Pre-Norman sculptured stones in Lancashire', LCAS 5, 1–18.

Bu'Lock, J.D., 1958, 'An east Scandinavian disc-brooch from Manchester', LCAS 67, 113–114.

Bunt, C. G. E. , 1930, 'The Lion and the Unicorn', Antiquity 4, 425–437.

Calverley, W.S., 1883, 'The sculptured cross at Gosforth, W. Cumberland', CW$_1$6, 373–404.

——, (ed. Collingwood, W.G.), 1899, *Notes on the early sculptured crosses, shrines and monuments in the present Diocese of Carlisle*, CWES XI, Kendal.

Campbell, A. (ed.), 1938, *The Battle of Brunanburh.*

Collingwood, W.G., 1899, 'The Ormside Cup', CW$_1$15, 381–387.

——, 1920, 'The Giant's Thumb', CW$_2$20, 53–65.

——, 1927, *Northumbrian crosses of the pre-Norman age.*

——,(ed.), see Calverley.

Combe, T., 1815, 'Account of some Saxon antiquities found near Lancaster', *Arch.* 17, 199–202.

Cowen, J.D., 1934, 'A catalogue of objects of the Viking period in the Tullie House Museum, Carlisle', CW$_2$34, 166–187.

——, 1948a, 'Viking burials in Cumbria', CW₂48, 73–76.

——, 1948b, 'A Viking sword from Eaglesfield near Cockermouth', AA4 26, 55–61.

——, 1967, 'Viking burials in Cumbria: a supplement', CW₂67, 31–34.

Crossley, J. (ed.), 1845, Pott's Discovery of Witches in the County of Lancaster, reprinted from the original edition of 1613, (Chetham Society vol. 6), Manchester.

Dickinson, S., 1985, 'Bryant's Gill, Kentmere: another 'Viking-period' Ribblehead ?', 83–88 in Baldwin and Whyte (eds) 1985.

Dodgson, J.McN., 1956–7, 'The background to Brunanburh', Saga Book of the Viking Club 14, 303–316.

Dunraven, Earl of, 1874, 'On an ancient chalice and brooches lately found at Ardagh', Trans. Roy. Irish Acad. 24, 433–454.

Edwards, B.J.N., 1970, 'The Claughton burial', HSLC 121, 109–116.

——,1984, 'Roman bone pins from the Curedale Hoard', Ant. Jul.,64, 365–366.

——, 1992, 'The Vikings in north-west England: the archaeological evidence', 43–62 in Graham Campbell (ed.) 1992.

——, 1997, 'A gold foil rediscovered', Contrebis 22, 11–12.

Evison, V.I., 1969, 'A Viking grave at Sonning, Berks.', Ant. Jnl. 49, 330–345.

Farrer, J.D. and Brownbill, J. (eds) 1902–1912, The Victoria History of the County of Lancaster, 8 vols.

Fell, C.I., 1956, 'A Viking spearhead from Kentmere', CW₂56, 67–69.

Ferguson, R.S., 1865, The Northmen in Cumberland and Westmorland, London and Carlisle.

——, 1891, 'Various finds in Ormside churchyard', CW₁15, 377–380.

Finberg, H.P.R. (ed.), see Wainwright.

Fishwick, H., 1891, The History of the parish of St Michael's-on-Wyre, (Chetham Society, N.S. vol. 25), Manchester.

Gaythorpe, H., 1910, 'The Rampside sword; with notes on the church and churchyard of Rampside in Furness', CW₂10, 298–306.

Graham-Campbell, J., 1995, The Viking-age gold and silver of Scotland, Edinburgh.

—— (ed.), 1992, Viking treasure from the north-west: the Cuerdale hoard in its context, Liverpool.

—— (ed.), see Philpott.

——, forthcoming, The Cuerdale Hoard and related Viking-Age silver from Britain and Ireland in the British Museum.

Grieg, S., 1947, 'Gjermundbufunnet', Norske Old-funn 8, 1–82.

Hall, R.A. (ed.), 1978, Viking age York and the north.

Henry, F., (1940) Irish art in the early Christian period.

Hodgson, C., (1832) 'An account of some antiquities found in a cairn, near Hesket-in-the-Forest in Cumberland ...', AA, 2, 106–109.

Hutton, F.R.C., 1901, 'Witherslack church and manor', CW₂1, 186–193.

Jansson, I., 1985, Ovala spännbucklor. En studie av vikingatida standardsmycken med utgångspunkt från Björkö-fynden. (Oval brooches. A study of viking period standard jewellery based on finds from Björkö (Birka), Sweden), Uppsala.

Johansen, O.S., 1973, 'Bossed penannular brooches: a systematization and study of their cultural affinities', Acta Archaeologia 44, 63–134.

Kendrick, T., 1941, 'The Viking taste in pre-Conquest England', Antiquity 15, 124–141.

King, A., 1978, 'Gauber High Pasture, Ribblehead – an interim report', 21–25 in Hall (ed.) 1978.

Kruse, S., 1986, 'The Viking silver hoard from Scotby: the non-numismatic element', CW₂86, 79–83.

Lidbetter, R.M., 'A pre-Norman shaft, recently found at Great Clifton church', CW₂ 2 108–112.

March, H.C., 1891, 'The pagan-Christian overlap in the north', LCAS 9, 49–89.

Mason, D.J.P, 1985, Excavations at Chester; 26–42, Lower Bridge Street, the Dark Age and Saxon periods, Chester.

Paulsen, P., 1953, Schwertortbänder der Wikinger-zeit, Stuttgart.

Pennant, T., 1790, A tour in Scotland and voyage to the Hebrides, MDCCLXXII, part I.

Philpott, F., 1990 (ed. Graham Campbell, J.), A silver saga: Viking treasure from the north-west, Liverpool.

Potter, T.W. and Andrews, R.D., 1994, 'Excavation and Survey at St Patrick's Chapel and St Peter's Church, Heysham, Lancashire, 1977–8', Ant. Jnl. 74, 55–134.

Raines, F.R., 1849, Notitia Cestriensis ... by the Right Rev. Francis Gastrell, D.D., Vol. II, part II (Chetham Society vol. 21), Manchester.

Richards, J.D., 1991, Viking Age England.

Rooke, H., 1792, 'Druidical and other British remains in Cumberland ...', *Arch.* 10, 105–113.

Ruding, R., 1840, *Annals of the British Coinage*,
3rd.ed.

Strudwick, J.S., 1858, 'Saxon and Arabic coins
found at Dean, Cumberland', BNJ 28, 177–180.

Thompson, J.D.A., 1956, *Inventory of British coin
hoards, A.D. 600–1500.*

Wainwright, F.T., 1948, 'Ingimund's invasion',
Eng. Hist. Rev. 63, 145–169.

——, 1975, *Scandinavian England: collected papers*
(ed. H.P.R. Finberg) Chichester.

Waterman, D.M., 1959, 'Late Saxon, Viking and
early medieval finds from York', *Arch.*97, 59–
105.

Watkin, W.T. 1883, *Roman Lancashire*, Liverpool.

Webster, G., 1953, 'A Saxon treasure hoard found
at Chester', *Ant. Jnl.* 33, 22–32.

Whitaker, J., 1775, *The History of Manchester*, vol. 2,
Post-Roman.

Whitaker, T.D., 1800, *An history ... of the ancient
parish of Whalley.*

White, R.H., 19??, 'Viking period sculpture at Neston, Cheshire', *Jnl. Chester Arch. Soc.* 69, 45–58.

Wilson, D.M., 1964, *Anglo-Saxon ornamental
metalwork, 700–1100, in the British Museum.*

——, 1967, 'The Vikings' relationship with Christianity in northern England', JBAA3 30, 37–46.

Yapp, B., 1990, 'The animals of the Ormside cup',
$CW_2$90, 147–161.

Youngs, S. (ed.), 1989, *'The work of angels': master-
pieces of Celtic metalwork, 6th–9th centuries* AD.

Abbreviations

AA$_1$,AA$_4$ – *Archaeologia Aeliana*, first and fourth series.
Arch. – Archaeologia.
BNJ – *British Numismatic Journal.*
CW$_1$, CW$_2$– *Transactions of the Cumberland and Westmorland Antiquarian and Archaeological Society*, first and second series.
CWES – Extra Series, Cumberland and Westmorland Antiquarian and Archaeological Society.

HSLC – *Transactions of the Historic Society of Lancashire and Cheshire.*
JBAA(3) – *Journal of the British Archaeological Association* (third series).
LCAS – *Transactions of the Lancashire and Cheshire Antiquarian Society.*
Trans. Roy. Irish Acad. – Transactions of the Royal Irish Academy.

Further Reading

Armstrong, A.M., Mawer, A., Stenton, F.M. and Dickins, B., 1950–1952, *The Place-Names of Cumberland* (English Place-Name Society vols XX-XXII), Cambridge.

Dodgson, J.McN., 1970–1981, *The Place-Names of Cheshire* (English Place-Name Society vols XLIV–XLVIII), Cambridge.

Ekwall, E., 1922, *The Place-Names of Lancashire* (Chetham Society vol. 81), Manchester.

Fellows Jensen, G., 1985a, *Scandinavia Settlement Names in the North-West* (Navnestudier XXV). Copenhagen.

——, 1985b, 'Scandinavian Settlement in Cumbria and Dumfriesshire: the Place-Name Evidence, pp. 65–82 in Baldwin and Whyte (eds) 1985.

Foote, P.G. and Wilson, D.M., 1970, *The Viking Achievement.*

Graham Campbell, J., 1980, *The Viking World.*

——, and Kydd, D., 1980, *The Vikings.*

Jones, G., 1968, *A History of the Vikings.*

Ritchie, A., 1993, *Viking Scotland.*

Roesdahl, E., Graham-Campbell, J., Connor, P. and Pearson, K. (eds), 1981, *The Vikings in England.*

Sawyer, P.H., 1971, *The Age of the Vikings.*

Smith, A.H., 1967, *The Place-Names of Westmorland* (English Place-Name Society vols XLII-XLIII), Cambridge.

Index

A main entry, if any, leads in bold; subsidiary mentions follow, succeeded by illustration pages in italics. English and Scottish counties (pre-1974) are abbreviated as follows: